SHORT WALKS FROM
Norfolk
Pubs

SHORT WALKS FROM
Norfolk Pubs

Liz Moynihan

COUNTRYSIDE BOOKS
NEWBURY, BERKSHIRE

First Published 1995
© Liz Moynihan 1995

COUNTRYSIDE BOOKS
3 Catherine Road
Newbury, Berkshire

ISBN 1 85306 340 1

To Rufus

Cover illustration by Colin Doggett
Photographs by the author
Maps by Sarah Talks

Produced through MRM Associates Ltd., Reading
Typeset by Paragon Typesetters, Queensferry, Clwyd
Printed by J. W. Arrowsmith Ltd., Bristol

Contents

Area map showing locations of the walks.

Publisher's Note

We hope that you obtain considerable enjoyment from this book; great care has been taken in its preparation. However, changes of landlord and actual closures are sadly not uncommon. Likewise, although at the time of publication all routes followed public rights of way or permitted paths, diversion orders can be made and permissions withdrawn.

We cannot of course be held responsible for such diversion orders and any inaccuracies in the text which result from these or any other changes to the routes, nor any damage which might result from walkers trespassing on private property. However, we are anxious that all details covering the walks and the pubs are kept up to date and would therefore welcome information from readers which would be relevant to future editions.

Introduction

Norfolk is one of the most diverse and interesting counties in Britain. It has a wealth of stately homes and parks, of splendid architecture and ancient ruins, of wildlife parks and museums in interesting places. Above all, it has lovely countryside – nothing extreme but an infinitely varied pattern of rolling fields, woods, commons, broads, marshes, cliffs and beaches. Many areas rich in flora and fauna are beautifully preserved by organisations such as the National Trust and the Norfolk Wildlife Trust, but in truth much of Norfolk is unspoilt – long may it last!

This book of pub walks is really a series of days out, linking a short walk with a visit to one or more of these special places, combined with a drink or a meal in a pleasant local pub. The aim was to find locations which appeal to all the family, of whatever age. Some walks have routes suitable for wheelchairs and pushchairs and whenever possible suggestions for longer walks are given.

It is useful to have the local Ordnance Survey Landranger map (1:50 000 series) with you to supplement the information given on the sketch maps accompanying each walk. This will show additional rights of way which can also be explored while in the area. It is worth mentioning that footpaths can easily become overgrown or churned up and the routes can also occasionally disappear over cultivated land. If you have difficulty telephone Norfolk County Council or the local district council, who have an obligation to sort things out. Do wear sensible footwear – either walking boots or wellingtons – because mud persists in some places even in dry spells and the ground is often rough and uneven. Please have the courtesy to take off muddy footwear in pubs, houses and museums.

It is usually possible to leave your car in the pub car park, but it is obviously only reasonable to do so if the establishment is going to receive your custom. Please notify the landlord if you intend to leave your car there for some time. The descriptions of the pubs give an indication of the kind of food served. This can vary enormously, but most pubs offer a very reasonable menu and some are positively gourmet! Details were accurate when going to press but, sadly, pubs often change hands and no responsibility can be accepted for any changes or differences. To be sure a pub is open and serving food at a time which is likely to suit you it is wise to phone first.

The places of interest suggested were all operational at the time of writing, and I hope they will continue to be so for a long time, because they reflect a tremendous range of interest and are well worth visiting. They will help you increase your enjoyment and understanding of Norfolk and that can only be a really good thing!

The Country Code should be observed at all times and is as follows:

Enjoy the countryside and respect its life and work.

Guard against all risk of fire.

Fasten all gates.

Keep dogs under close control.

Keep to public paths across farmland.

Use gates and stiles to cross fences, hedges and walls.

Take your litter home.

Help to keep all water clean.

Protect wildlife, plants and trees.

Take special care on country roads.

Make no unnecessary noise.

I hope you enjoy the hospitality of the chosen pubs and my selection of the footpaths and byways of this lovely county.

Liz Moynihan
Spring 1995

1 Morston
The Anchor

This is an intriguing old pub which has been in the same family for over 100 years and not a lot has changed in that time. The snug, the original tap room, is old fashioned, having a motley collection of furniture with plenty of cushions sprinkled about and a roaring wood fire in winter. A new bar, complete with piano, has been built onto one side while on the other is the office where Temple's Ferry Service offers trips to Blakeney Harbour. There is no garden but one or two tables and a row of stools stand on the forecourt outside.

The food on offer is fairly simple. There is a wide variety of sandwiches, crab salads and a few hot snacks. Coffee, tea and cakes are also available. Children are welcome and have their own menu, or small portions are offered. The serving of food tends to fit round the busy time of the high tides when the ferries go out, but no food is served in the evening. As for drinks, Flowers Bitter and Heineken lager are on draught. The pub is open each day and all day in the summer holidays and keeps normal pub hours at other times.

Telephone: 01263 740791.

How to get there: The Anchor is in the middle of Morston village on the main A149 coast road, a mile or so west of Blakeney.

Parking: There is limited parking outside the pub. The National Trust provide a large pay and display car park, lookout and information centre down near Morston Quay.

Length of the walk: 2 miles, or more if the walk is extended along the high bank to the east towards Blakeney (Norfolk Coast Path). OS Landranger map 133 North East Norfolk (inn GR 008439).

Morston salt marsh is an enchanting expanse of wide open space. A mixture of muddy creeks and pools intersect the varied salt marsh vegetation, purple with sea lavender in summer. The marshes are edged with shingle and sand dunes merging into Blakeney channel, which divides the Morston saltings from the sandhills of Blakeney Point across the water. There is a forest of masts wherever you look and on the landward side are lovely views of Blakeney and Morston churches. This walk explores the quay and the saltings and should only be undertaken at low tide (see tide table at the information centre) as some of the tracks can be under water at certain stages. The height of the tide varies at different times of the year and the walk can be very muddy – wellington boots or bare feet are recommended.

The Walk
Turn left out of the pub and walk carefully along the road to the corner. Opposite Morston Hall Hotel is a small green with a circular seat round a tree. Take the stony track leading away from the road, signposted to Morston Quay. A left fork leads to the car park, but continue ahead past public lavatories towards the sea bank. At the 'Coast Path' signpost, bear left along the track towards the information centre. Carry on past this to the stone cairn donation box. Bear right on to a hard area of mud (Morston Quay). A deep creek lies to the right, where the ferries, fishing boats and pleasure craft can moor. Continue along the edge of the creek and cross a wooden bridge over a small inlet at the end of the hard. Bear right towards a larger wooden bridge, cross it and continue on along the edge of the creek towards a third wooden bridge. Go over yet another large bridge. The creek winds away to the right here, but the walk continues straight on, following the well-worn mud path which snakes through the marsh, more or less ahead. There are good views now of the channel which leads to Blakeney, lined with large yachts at anchor.

At a slightly higher grassy area, bear left along an obvious path. The path which leads ahead goes further on into the marshes and peters out. Enjoy the superb views over to Blakeney Point on the right and the pine woods of Wells and Holkham ahead. The path is now wide

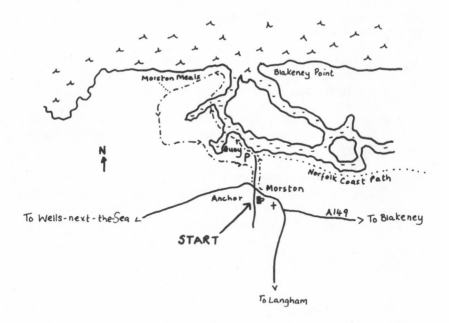

and stony, then sandy, continuing in a gentle curve towards the left. As you come off the slightly higher ground the path divides into two muddy tracks. Take the right-hand one, which negotiates several small creeks (just a step over) to reach the sand and shingle area of Morston Meals. Here you feel miles from anywhere. I have memories of a sunny day when the sea was brilliant blue beyond the purple stripes of lavender and the yellow stripes of sand. A large party of swans was idling in the creek. The only humans were fishermen walking out to collect cockles, mussels or bait from the shallows. The path ends at a marshy area, with a large creek on the left.

After exploring this area, turn back the way you came to where the paths divided and this time take the left-hand, muddy path. This starts off as quite a broad track through the marsh and now heads almost directly back inland. The path crosses various creeky areas. Jump them and carry on. The path bears right to a higher area of dunes. Another track goes off to the left, but go on a little way and then bear left down the obvious track (there are various other paths here but the general idea is to bear left to quite a big, rutted track and continue ahead again, inland).

You will meet a broad, grassy cross track through gorse and scrub. This is the coast path. Turn left along this. Again, there are various paths leading in the same direction. Keep along the main one, cross over a hump which is part of the sea defences and continue on towards a pantiled house ahead. Turn left up steps over the sea wall (arrow marker). On the other side bear right and continue on to join the main gravelly cross track. Bear left along this towards the information centre and just past where some scrubby trees come in between parked boats an arrow points the coast path up and over the bank and along the edge of the car park, back to the gravel track that leads in from the main road. Turn right up the track and retrace your steps to the pub.

Places of interest nearby

Boat trips go to *Blakeney Harbour* to see seals or to land on the nature reserve of *Blakeney Point*. Temple's ferries are bookable at the Anchor pub (01263 740791) or Bean's Boat Trips can be booked from 12, The Street, Morston (01263 740038). *Blakeney Harbour Sailing*, based at Morston, offers sailing lessons or charter trips on locally built boats. Telephone: 01263 740377. *Langham Glass*, a mile or two inland, is housed in various lovely 18th century barns, where a viewing gallery allows you to watch glass being blown. There is a factory shop, an adventure playground, a video room and a licensed tearoom. Telephone: 01328 830511.

2 Burnham Thorpe
The Lord Nelson

This cream-washed cottage pub dates back to the 1650s and very little has changed since then. In Nelson's day it was known as the Plough but it was renamed in 1807, two years after his death. As in its early days, the beer – all real ale – is served straight from the casks in the ground floor cellar. This is certainly an attraction and makes it a pub with a difference. Greene King IPA, Abbot and Mild and Woodforde's Nelson's Revenge are on offer. You will also find Greene King Winter Ale in season, Guinness, Harp lager and Red Rock cider. An unusual 'bone warmer' is a mug of hot chocolate with cream and a flake. The food is fairly standard pub grub and includes a useful English breakfast. The HMS Sizzler is a gargantuan mixed grill, while at the other extreme is an excellent home-made soup. There are vegetarian meals and a specials board. The children's menu has six choices.

The Wardroom is a no-smoking room with a tiled floor, velvet curtains and simple tables and chairs. It has a mural of the battle of Trafalgar and Nelson pictures on the walls. The Nelson room has high backed settles and a friendly atmosphere. There are open fires in winter. Various games are on offer and a football net awaits goals in the garden. The pub keeps normal opening hours in winter but in the summer season it stays open daily from 11 am to 11 pm, with cold food all day.

Telephone: 01328 738421.

How to get there: Turn off the A149 coast road between Hunstanton and Wells-next-the-Sea to Burnham Market, then take the B1355 Fakenham road, turning almost immediately left off it to reach Burnham Thorpe. The Lord Nelson is in the middle of the village opposite the recreation ground.

Parking: The pub has its own parking.

Length of the walk: 3½ miles or there is a shorter circuit of the village on lanes suitable for wheelchairs or pushchairs. OS Landranger map 132 North West Norfolk (inn GR 852418).

Nelson was born in Burnham Thorpe, where his father was rector, and after he was married, he lived in the village for five years, holding a leaving party in the pub before taking command of a new ship, the Agamemnon, in 1793. The walk explores the beautiful, undulating countryside surrounding the little river Burn — views that Nelson would have known so well — and takes in the various sites in the village that are linked with him.

Burnham Thorpe church.

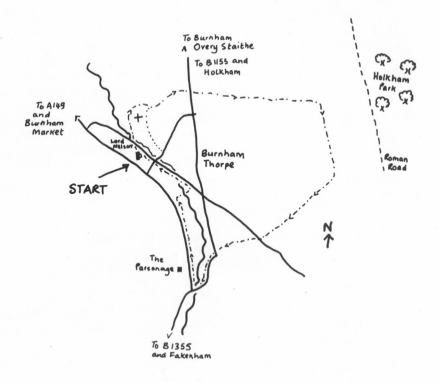

The Walk

Turn left out of the pub and walk along the lane alongside the river on the right. Pass a lovely old farm and huge barn on the left. Take a little fork to the right, signposted to the church, and continue on towards the Manor House, which stands on an ancient moated site. The road crosses the river and soon bears right. Ignore the footpath turning left into a humpy field and continue bearing right past a copse, then take a left turn up a broad, stony path, which curves round uphill with a field on the right and the copse on the left.

The lane ahead passing the church returns to the village – a short cut for wheelchairs and pushchairs.

The track curves round to a tiny lane. Cross this and continue on ahead up the track. The countryside is fringed with stands of trees and ahead is the lovely mixed woodland of Holkham Hall, where a Roman road runs along the boundary wall. However, our route turns off before reaching this, veering right by an old flint barn. The track passes the end of a group of trees, with a footpath signposted off to the right. Ignore this and continue on to a wooden public footpath signpost at the end of a scrappy hedge on the left. Turn right here and follow the wide track downhill. A lovely panorama of fields, hedges and trees stretches out ahead. Pass a ruined barn on the left and wind downhill. The track crosses a small road. Turn right for a short cut back to Burnham Thorpe.

The main walk continues on down the track as it curves to right and left. The track comes out onto another small road. Turn left along this avoiding the track to the left. There are views of The Parsonage over the field on the right. Follow the road as it curves to the right, ignoring a track off on the left. Cross over the river and turn right at a road junction, signposted to Nelson's birthplace.

On one side of the road is the river, on the other is the old wall in front of The Parsonage, into which is set a plaque commemorating Nelson's birth. The stream bears off through the field on the right. Continue on along the road. A fairly short distance after a long house on the right watch out for a public footpath signpost by a stile. Cross this to the right and walk through a meadow along a boundary fence to cross another stile and a plank footbridge over the stream. Go over a small piece of rough ground and walk across the middle of the field ahead, making for a huge old tree, just beyond which is a stile (footpath signpost) leading onto a lane.

Turn left and walk along the lane (Walsingham Road), passing attractive brick and flint cottages and houses. The stream meets the road again on the left by a Primitive Methodist chapel of 1864, which has a little bridge over the stream. The road now crosses the stream, which flows on the right-hand side. Ignore a byroad to the left and go on to a staggered crossroads by the village sign. Burnham Overy Staithe is signposted 2½ miles to the right. Continue straight on, passing more pretty cottages, back to the pub.

Places of interest nearby

The beautiful church of *All Saints*, where Nelson's parents and brother and sister are buried (Nelson himself is in St Paul's cathedral), has Nelson memorabilia including a cross and a lectern made from wood from HMS Victory. Nelson's memorial bust is on the wall of the chancel. Nearby *Burnham Market* is a perfect little market town with interesting shops surrounding a wide green, and at *Burnham Overy Staithe* you can walk out to empty sandy beaches along the sea wall. *Holkham Hall* is an 18th century Palladian mansion set in a 3,000 acre deer park, with a museum, a pottery and a garden centre among other attractions. Telephone: 01328 710227.

3 Upper Sheringham
The Red Lion

This simple pub, part of a terrace of cobblestone cottages, provides a warm welcome for all. The main bar has a tiled floor, a woodburning stove and is simply furnished with old pine settles and tables and chairs. There is also a no-smoking room which has lovely time-worn boards on the floor, a stripped pine wainscot and a huge beam – all reputed to have come from ships wrecked at sea. Boules and croquet can be played in the large garden at the back, almost hidden behind outhouses (one once a blacksmith's forge) and overlooking the interesting churchyard. There are two bed and breakfast rooms with sea views.

Reputed to have the deepest cellar in Norfolk, the pub (a freehouse) serves four excellent real ales – Bateman, Adnams bitter, Woodforde's Norfolk and Wherry – and has a huge stock of malt whiskies (there is always a 'Malt of the Month' on offer). A full wine list is available. The food is delicious and local seafood, game and meat are much in evidence, though vegetarians also have plenty of choice. The traditional puddings are all home-baked. A board offers a set two-course menu and on Wednesday nights the chef goes 'Round the World' with a specially cooked three-course meal from different countries. On Saturdays there is usually mustard-glazed hot baked ham, and on Sundays traditional roasts of rib of beef and pork. The pub keeps normal hours but closes on Sunday evenings during winter. Telephone: 01263 825408.

How to get there: Upper Sheringham can be reached through Sheringham on the A149 coast road or is signposted off the A148 between Holt and Cromer. The Red Lion is in the middle of the village, not far from the church.

Parking: There is a car park opposite the pub or spaces can be found near the church. Parking for Pretty Corner woods is on the A1082 on the outskirts of Sheringham or near where the A1082 joins the A148. There is a pay and display car park for Sheringham Park off the A148.

Length of the walk: 2 miles (or longer options round Sheringham Park). OS Landranger map 133 North East Norfolk (inn GR 145419).

Norfolk is not renowned for its hills, but this walk, which is fairly close to the highest point of the county at West Runton, does have some fairly steep elevations and lovely views towards the cliffs and sea. Upper Sheringham is unspoilt and the

Cottages, Upper Sheringham.

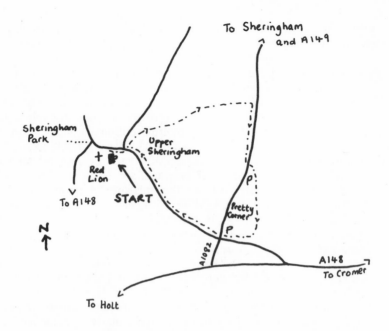

mix of cobbled and pantiled cottages and houses is particularly attractive against a backdrop of fields and mixed woodland. The walk goes through some of the beautiful woods at Pretty Corner and longer tracks can be taken here. Nearby Sheringham Park offers all the delights of walking in a landscaped park with spectacular views of the sea.

The Walk

Turn right out of the pub and walk a little way to a junction of roads. Go ahead up Cranfield Road and almost immediately turn left along a wide farm track, passing a gate on the left into a farmyard. The track goes through fields rising to woods on the right. This track is called The Butts – a good place to stand and shoot high pheasants driven out of the wood. Pass housing on the left behind hedging and come out onto a main road on the outskirts of Sheringham.

Turn right up the road to the 30 mph delimit sign by the woods. Soon after this, on the left, is a car park in which there is an information board showing walking routes of different lengths. For this walk take the broad track going rightish uphill through the woods, passing a log barrier. When the track forks, follow the right-hand branch, going steeply uphill until it meets a cross track with a marker post on the junction. Carry on ahead up the main track, ignoring the branch which curves off to the left. At another marker post by a junction of tracks bear right again to a further car park and information board. Go ahead out of the entrance to the car park, onto a little lane with another marker post on the left.

Turn right down the lane, cross a more main road and take the single track road, signposted to Upper Sheringham. This is the other end of Cranfield Road, a most attractive old hollow lane which meanders downhill through trees. Ignore a track to the left and continue on down the lane. Pass attractive cobbled cottages and a farm on the right with some lovely old barns. Pass the track taken on the outward journey and at the junction of lanes continue on back to the pub, passing the post office and general stores on the left.

To extend the walk, carry on past the pub and All Saints' church. The latter is well worth a visit, with its 15th century rood screen and loft and some lovely carved bench ends. Outside is an unusual drinking water reservoir, with an inscription recording the first peace of the Napoleonic Wars. Continue on ahead, ignoring the left turn going uphill. Pass Weybourne Road to the right and carry on ahead down a lane to a pedestrian entrance to Sheringham Park, where a map shows the main walks within these 770 acres of glorious parkland, landscaped by Humphrey Repton. The park, which is open to walkers from sunrise to sunset, is particularly spectacular at rhododendron and azalea time. The house is not open to the public except by written appointment.

Places of interest nearby

The North Norfolk Railway (the mainly steam-driven Poppy Line) runs from Sheringham via Weybourne to Holt through beautiful countryside. There is a visitors' centre and museum, souvenir shop and buffet at Sheringham. Telephone: 01263 822045. *The Muckleburgh Collection* of military vehicles at Weybourne is 2 miles away. Telephone: 01263 70210. Another mile further on is the *East Anglian Falconry Centre* at Kelling. Telephone: 01263 712235.

4 Little Walsingham
The Bull

All shapes and shades of pilgrim have been through the door of this 15th century pub down through the years. The building has been sympathetically stripped back to its ancient state, revealing old beams, masonry and inglenooks. The furnishings are in keeping and the devilish-looking pitchfork on the bar is handy if pilgrims become unruly, like some from the past who set fire to the pub because they felt they had been overcharged. A beam in the lounge bar bears evidence of old charring. Here a collection of several hundred priest's calling cards sent from all over the world are pinned to the beams – would Queen Victoria, who looks down on it all from the wall, have approved?

At the back is a sheltered beer garden where summertime customers can sit at umbrella-shaded tables, admiring the huge hollyhocks, with pots of geraniums abounding. The outside walls of the pub are clad in all manner of climbing plants, including the old fashioned rose, Rambling Rector. Tables at the front, where customers can enjoy a beer while watching the busy scene in Common Place, are shaded by an old maple tree. Bar food is served at the usual times, but in the winter evening meals may only be served at weekends. The menu is

small and simple, though Holy Smoke sounds exciting – flaked smoked haddock in a creamy cheese sauce – while St Peter's Platter is a dish of peppered mackerel, crab sticks, prawns and salad. There is a specials board and a roast on Sundays. The pub keeps normal drinking hours and serves Burton and Tolly Original real ales. There are three lagers on draught, as well as Tetley Bitter, Guinness, Whitbread Poacher Bitter and Mild. Dry Blackthorn is the cider.
Telephone: 01328 820333.

How to get there: Little Walsingham is on the B1105 half way between Fakenham and Wells. Follow this road which becomes the High Street and turn into Common Place where the Bull is situated.

Parking: There is limited parking in the square outside, but a large pay and display car park lies just up an alley leading from Common Place, with vehicle access off Guild Street.

Length of the walk: 3½ miles. OS Landranger map 132 North West Norfolk (inn GR 934369).

The importance of Little Walsingham as a place of pilgrimage down the centuries and the wealth of interesting old ruins and sites here and in the surrounding countryside have lent a very special aura to the whole area. The walk passes the Anglo-Catholic shrine, the Augustinian priory and the friary, as well as interesting secular buildings such as the Shirehall museum, the town pump, and the old Bridewell prison (in the car park) which closed in 1831. A cross-country walk, with views of rolling countryside laced with ancient ecclesiastical ruins, leads to Great Walsingham, a beautiful, sleepy backwater, where the walker crosses the river Stiffkey at a pretty ford before ambling back to the larger village of Little Walsingham.

The Walk
Leave the Bull and go ahead up Common Place, passing the town pump on the left. Turn right along Bridewell Street by the entrance to the car park. Turn left at the T-junction opposite the Robin Hood pub and walk up to the start of the Wells and Walsingham Railway on the right. Turn left opposite this, along a wide roadway leading to a coach park. Pass the former station on the left, now a chapel. Continue onto the wide track of the old railway. On the left are views over Walsingham and the old friary. Shortly you come to a crossing of tracks.

Turn left off the old railway and go down a broad, stony track between hedges to a narrow lane. Turn left along this (more views of the friary ruins). The lane comes to houses, with flint walls much in evidence. At a crossroads turn right down Station Road which leads into Friday Market at the Black Lion hotel.

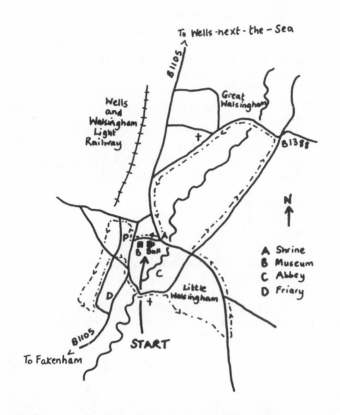

To Wells-next-the-Sea

B1105

Wells
and
Walsingham
Light
Railway

Great
Walsingham

B1388

Wells and Walsingham Light Railway

N

A Shrine
B Museum
C Abbey
D Friary

P

A

B

C

D

Little
Walsingham

B1105

To Fakenham

START

A short cut back to the pub is possible at this point. Turn left and go up the High Street past cafés and shops to the 15th century gatehouse leading into the priory.

The main walk turns right through Friday Market with its lovely old buildings, to come out via a lane onto the lower end of the High Street. Turn right and then almost immediately bear left down Church Street, which is bounded by the high walls of the Abbey on the left, and cross the little river Stiffkey to reach the church of St Mary. Bear left here and then right up the drive to Abbey Farm. Just before a wooden gate near farm buildings, turn left over a stile and go ahead across the middle of a meadow towards a hollow dip, where there is another stile to the right of a gate. Cross this and continue on (with a wood on the right), soon bearing right across the next field towards a stile a short way to the left of a metal gate. Cross this and go left to the road. Turn left. After the Little Walsingham sign, turn left at a road junction (old pillbox on right) and walk along a lane through woods to a crossroads.

For a short cut leading back to Little Walsingham continue on ahead.

For the main route, turn right and carry on along the road into Great Walsingham and at a junction of roads (Methodist chapel of 1895, now a Russian Orthodox church, on the right), turn left, signposted 'Unbridged Ford'. Go over the pedestrian bridge by the ford. Pass Tudor Berry Hall with its crow stepped gables, on the left, and at a pretty green where three ways meet, bear left up tiny St Peter's Lane, passing the fine 14th century church on the right. Follow the lane back down into Little Walsingham. Turn left at the main road and go down into the village, continuing on at another road junction to pass the shrine. Turn right at the junction here to return to the pub.

Places of interest nearby

The Shrine of Our Lady of Walsingham was originally built by the lady of the manor in 1061 and became an important place of pilgrimage in medieval times, with pilgrims' hostels being built nearby. In this century the new shrine was built and a Roman Catholic shrine was established at the Slipper Chapel in Houghton St Giles a few miles away. The *Shirehall Museum* (and tourist information centre) was built in the early 16th century as an important hostel and was then converted, with a Georgian façade, into a venue for the Quarter

Little Walsingham.

Sessions. It is now a museum, with the Georgian courtroom as its centrepiece. An excellent guide to the Walsinghams can be bought here. Telephone: 01328 820510. The important Augustinian priory (*the Abbey*) was founded in the 12th century but little remains of the original buildings except the west tower and the east gable end of the church. In the atmospheric wooded grounds are some holy wells and the medieval pack-horse bridge over the river Stiffkey. The *Franciscan Friary* was founded in the 14th century. Part of the walling of the church chancel still survives and the domestic ruins are some of the finest in Norfolk. The *Wells to Walsingham Narrow Gauge Railway* runs throughout the summer. Timetable from the Shirehall museum.

5 Snettisham
The Rose and Crown

Ever since the 14th century this white-painted, flower-hung pub has been devoted to looking after people's every need. At the front of the building are two cosy, beamed rooms linked by a long copper bar. One has an old fashioned penny seat – throw all twelve pennies in and you win a bottle of whisky. The other is pretty and snug, with cushioned benches and frilly flowery curtains. The back bar has unusual seating made from beer barrels, while the restaurant is an attractive mixture of pews and old wood tables and chairs with a collection of nostalgic pictures adorning the walls. Families are given special consideration and will find a purpose-built barbecue room which opens onto a partially-paved, walled garden with the special attraction of an aviary, various caged animals and an excellent playground, including a wooden fort, a Wendy house and a sand pit. There is wheelchair access and nappy changing facilities, but no dogs are allowed. Bed and breakfast is available.

The pub has a good reputation for its food and its standard menu is very comprehensive, including a large section for vegetarians. There are indoor barbecue meals as well as a large menu for children. Specials are shown on a blackboard and could include such things as haddock cheese and ham shantie (fish in a cheese and ham sauce with breadcrumbs). The home-made meringue glacé is renowned. As a freehouse, the pub goes to town on its real ales, which include Adnams, Bass, IPA, Abbot and its own Rose and Crown ale. Sometimes there is an unusual guest ale and the list of other beers is extensive. Three lagers are on draught – Tennent's Extra and Pilsner, and Carling Black Label, as well as Dry Blackthorn cider. The pub prides itself on its wine list and offers specials each week. Freshly squeezed orange juice is to be found too. The hours for food and for drinking are the usual ones, except that the pub stays open from 11 am to 11 pm on Saturdays.

Telephone: 01485 541382.

How to get there: Snettisham is signposted off the A149 bypass, just south of Heacham. The Rose and Crown is in Old Church Road, a turning off the main street near the centre of the village.

Parking: There is plenty of space behind the Rose and Crown and some parking in the village square nearby.

Length of the walk: 3½ miles. OS Landranger map 132 North West Norfolk (inn GR 686342).

This walk goes through a typical Norfolk farming landscape to the outskirts of the interesting village of Ingoldisthorpe. A detour could be taken to explore the village before returning to the route of the walk, which descends a valley to follow the little river Ingol before turning up towards Snettisham again through the grounds of Park Farm, with its deer and farm animals as well as archaeological sites.

The Walk

Many of the local buildings are made from rich brown carr stone which has been quarried in Snettisham for centuries. To view the quarry, which is still in action, turn right out of the pub and walk along between old lime trees and the old carr stone wall which surrounds the lovely Old Hall (dating from the time of William and Mary), which is now a Sue Ryder home. At the main road turn right along the pavement to reach a bend. Continue on with care for a few yards and then branch right up a broad, stony track. Ignore the public footpath which filters to the right and continue to the top of the track where it meets a cross track next to the quarry beyond the hedge. Bear right here and follow the track round towards what looks like a private garden. At a junction of paths near cottages turn left, passing Norton Hill Lodge on the right, and go ahead to a wooden gate. Go through the kissing gate next to this (footpath signpost) and go over a small

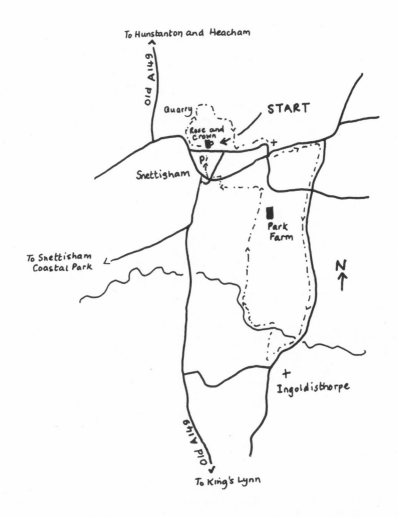

To Hunstanton and Heacham

Old A149

Quarry

START

Rose and Crown

Snettisham

P

Park Farm

To Snettisham Coastal Park

N

+ Ingoldisthorpe

Old A149

To King's Lynn

piece of meadow here towards a gate in fencing. Go through a small wooden gate to the right of this, cross a piece of well-kept grass to another kissing gate to the right of a wooden gate, with a footpath signpost pointing back. Go through and continue down the drive of Hall Farm through another large wooden gate. At the bottom of the drive ignore another path to the left and carry on to the road, turning left up it to the church.

This first section of the walk can be left out, in which case turn left out of the pub and continue up the road to the splendid church with its medieval stone spire. Follow the road as it bears right round the church and then at a crossroads take the left turn, signposted to Sedgeford. The road ahead leads to Park Farm. Carry on to where the road bends to the left and take the tiny lane leading to the right here through arable fields. Continue ahead at the crossroads. Park Farm buildings are on the right. Continue for some distance down this lane. After crossing a stream almost hidden in bushes the lane goes uphill, passing a house on the left on the outskirts of Ingoldisthorpe. Opposite a driveway a kissing gate goes into a meadow. Turn right into this and go diagonally across towards a stile in a fence, in line with Snettisham church tower soaring above the trees. Cross the stile and continue diagonally across the next, uneven, field to a footbridge. Cross this and turn left along the stream, following its curves to another footbridge on the left. Ignore this and continue on to a third footbridge. Cross this and go through a metal kissing gate into a field (marker post). Follow the fence on the left for a little way and then continue on across the middle of the field, guided by another marker post showing the route. Continue on towards cottages ahead, passing the site of a Roman villa near a copse on the right. Go through another gate near the cottages (footpath signpost). Do a quick right turn then turn left along a broad farm path, aiming straight at the church. We are now within the curtilage of Park Farm.

Where the track veers off to the right, go ahead through a metal gate (footpath signpost) by a little carr stone barn and carry on towards the church. When the stone wall here ends keep on along fencing (ignoring gates and arrows which refer to the Park Farm complex) towards a large tree. Go through a metal kissing gate onto a drive, turn left over some grass and go down a little twitchel. This path comes out onto Manor Lane and reaches a more main road. Bear right here and come to an even bigger road near a playing field. Turn left, passing the Victorian school adorned with a bell tower. When the road bends to the left continue straight ahead down a no through road, passing a rather splendid old carr stone factory. Go through bollards onto the main road. Bear immediately towards the right up an alleyway, with the Old Bank Coffee and Teashop on the left, passing cottages to reach Old Church Road. Turn right to the pub.

Places of interest nearby

Park Farm, a working farm, provides an excellent day out with its deer safari, farm animals, pony rides, craft workshops and adventure playground. There are three walking trails, including a 2½ mile archaeological one sponsored by English Heritage. Telephone: 01485 542425. Also in Snettisham on the road leading to the marshes and sea

Snettisham church.

is a working *watermill* dating from 1800. It is open on Wednesday and Thursday in season and home-milled flour can be bought. Actually at the sea is the 143 acre wildlife refuge of *Snettisham Coastal Park*, as well as the 3,250 acre RSPB *Snettisham Reserve*, with its mud flats and brackish lagoons, which is excellent for wading birds and wildfowl. At nearby Heacham is *Caley Mill* the home of Norfolk Lavender. A guided tour is available in season but the grounds, gift shop and tea room are open all year round, except Christmas.

6 Thursford
The Crawfish

At the turn of the century, when the railway came through here, the Crawfish was built to take over the sustenance of travellers from the Old Crawfish, which was a coaching inn on the turnpike road nearby. Now, although it is a little way out of Thursford, it acts as an excellent village local as well as catching passing trade. Inside, the pub is pleasantly old fashioned and has roaring fires in winter. The separate dining room has a Victorian theme. Customers can sit on the old bench or tables outside the front door to view the passing scene, and there are a few tables in the small garden. Exuberant baskets of flowers hang from the glass roofed verandah throughout the summer.

The landlord does the cooking and offers a different menu at lunchtime and in the evening. There is a special children's menu, or small portions can be offered. The daily special is advertised on a board and on Sundays there is traditional roast beef or occasionally lamb. The meat is local and very good. There are three vegetarian meals on offer, including hazlenut and mushroom roast. The lunch menu includes traditional pub food, but the evening menu may include specials such as home-cooked braised steak and onions. The opening and food serving hours are pretty standard. Real ales offered are Tolly Original and Flowers, while Guinness, Murphy's stout, Whitbread Mild and Tetley Bitter are all on draught. Castlemaine XXXX and Carlsberg are the draught lagers and the cider is Dry Blackthorn.

Telephone: 01328 878313.

How to get there: Thursford is signposted off the A148 between Fakenham and Holt. The Crawfish stands on a crossroads a few hundred yards from the turn.

Parking: There is some parking at the pub or cars can be left in the car park of the Thursford Collection if you intend to visit it.

Length of the walk: About 2½ miles. OS Landranger map 132 North West Norfolk (inn GR 994339).

Thursford is a scattering of pretty cottages and the Elizabethan Old Hall, a remnant of a Tudor manor house, is set near the church in wooded estate farmland. The walk links this hamlet with the slightly larger village of Thursford Green, which is home to the Thursford Collection of old steam road engines and colourful mechanical organs. The views from the lush, green lanes are delightful. An extension to the walk leads to Thursford Wood, which contains some extremely ancient oak trees.

Thursford church.

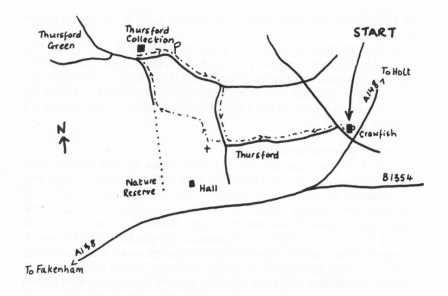

The Walk

Turn right out of the pub and walk down the road, shortly turning left down a small lane (Heath Lane) which passes through fields backing onto woods and is lined with banks of wildflowers in summer. The lane passes a few cottages and bears right at a grassy triangle with a post box. Turn left soon down a wide track, signposted to Thursford Old Hall. The church with its sheep-cropped churchyard is well worth a visit and further on down the track you can get a better view of the Hall.

However, the route of the walk turns right before the church up a grassy concessionary path, passing between a treed hedgerow and a young copse. At a cross track (Clark's Lane) turn left. There are lovely views over the church and the Tudor chimneys of the Hall from this broad, green way.

The walk can be extended by an extra mile by passing a farm building on the left and then, at a junction of paths, turning left and continuing down the track to Thursford Wood near the main road.

For the main walk, at the junction of tracks turn right up another broad, stony track, which eventually reaches the houses of Thursford Green and emerges onto the attractive, tree-shaded green with its interesting village sign. Turn right along the main road through the village, passing the former school on the right and the buildings of the Thursford Collection on the left. Further on is the entrance to the car park.

At the next small crossroads turn right down a small lane signposted to Thursford church and carry on past the beginning of grassy Clark's Lane on the right. Pass the track leading to the church on the right and retrace your steps, bearing left into Heath Lane with its view of Barney church over the fields to the right. Turn right again at the main road to reach the pub.

Places of interest nearby

At the *Thursford Collection* you can ride on an old roundabout with Venetian gondolas, old farm buildings house the Thursford shops, and refreshments are served in a timbered barn or a garden conservatory opening onto lawns. There is daily live musical entertainment featuring the organs, including the Mighty Wurlitzer, from April to the end of October and again at Christmas. Telephone: 01328 878477. *Thursford Wood* (Norfolk Wildlife Trust) is a remnant of medieval wood pasture containing some of the oldest oak trees in the county, which support an amazing variety of wildlife. A pond encourages water birds and in spring the woods are ablaze with rhododendrons.

Castle Rising
The Black Horse

This Beefeater pub provides an excellent service in very comfortable surroundings. Through the main door with its stained glass panel, a carpeted lobby leads left into a large rectangular bar comfortably furnished with deep sofas and well upholstered benches complemented by richly coloured carpets and curtains. It has a feature fireplace in one corner where a fire is lit in winter. The samplers and pictures on the walls and the old salt glaze pots standing around are all carefully chosen to enhance the feeling of Victorian comfort. To the right, down steps, is an interesting restaurant area which seats 92 people, but in small intimate sections. Here, again, the pretty Victorian fireplace, chintzy curtains and old bits and pieces strengthen the period theme. A grassy area outside has tables, while an exciting children's play area with a deep bark safety surface is near the old stables. The toilets have baby changing facilities.

The bar offers Flower's Original, Marston's Pedigree, Abbot, Boddingtons Bitter and Old Speckled Hen and sometimes an extra guest ale. Stella Artois and Heineken lagers are on draught as well as Murphy's Irish stout and Whitbread Best Bitter. Morning coffee is served. The bar is open all day for bar food from 11 am. The snacks include baguettes with five different fillings, including pastrami beef and tikka mayonnaise, while a special might be satisfying Hungarian goulash. The restaurant with its comprehensive menu and special children's Mister Men menu operates from 12 noon to 2.30 pm and from 6 pm to 10.30 pm except on Sundays when it is open all day. There is a good wine list.

Telephone: 01553 631225.

How to get there: Castle Rising is just off the A149 road to Hunstanton, a few miles north of King's Lynn. Follow the one way system as you approach the village then at a crossroads in the centre turn right to reach the Black Horse.

Parking: There is a large pub car park and a car park with toilets at the castle during its opening hours.

Length of the walk: 2½ miles (short cuts possible). OS Landranger map 132 North West Norfolk (inn GR 666248).

The views from the castle earthworks over the Wash and the surrounding countryside are spectacular, while at ground level this gentle walk winds past woods, fields and streams before exploring the many delights of the historic village of Castle Rising, once a sea port before the entrance to the river silted up.

The Walk

Turn right out of the main door of the pub, then right again down a lane alongside the post office/shop/tearoom, passing the lovely old lamp, a memorial to the First World War. Further on pass a gate to the interesting Norman church of St Lawrence and follow the curve of the lane left to a beautiful village green with an old market cross shaded by mature lime trees. Continue on the road as it bears right, ignoring a left turn leading to modern houses. On the corner here is a little old carr stone reading room with a rustic porch. At a T-junction at the bottom, turn right. The road to the left goes to Wootton Carr. This walk goes to the right along a gravelly lane to Night Marsh, bearing left shortly, near a public footpath.

For a short cut take this footpath to the right through parkland to come out onto another lane on the other side of the church.

To continue on the main route, walk to the left down this wide and pleasant lane. Where the lane bends sharply to the left, turn right (footpath signpost) and walk along the edge of a big field. This is Night Marsh with a view of ruined St Felix church in the distance. The track bears right and climbs to a lane.

For another short cut follow this to the right back to the village.

For the main walk turn left along the lane, passing through fields intersected by drainage ditches – the wild flowers are excellent along here. Just before a bridge near Day Common, turn right and walk along the banks of the Babingley river on the left. The path comes out at the busy A149. Cross carefully and go down a bank over a stile into a marshy meadow. Follow along the river to a large beech tree and then cross the meadow right to a signposted stile by wooden gates. Here at a crossroads of drives go straight across (see the footpath signpost), passing two cottages on the right. At the end of a garden by a conifer hedge a signpost on the right indicates two paths. Take the right-hand one through woodland (this may be rather overgrown). Cross a bridge over a murky stream and follow the path on its slightly wiggly course, passing along a kind of causeway with shallow ditches on either side. Cross another plank bridge and go on up the bank and over a fence to the A149 again (footpath signpost).

Cross to a signpost and go ahead through the middle of a field along a wide track left between crops. At a baulk keep to the left-hand side

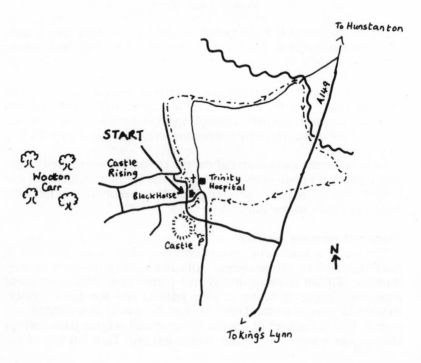

Castle at Castle Rising.

and continue ahead along the edge of a field on the right. The houses of Castle Rising and the castle itself come into view. Walk past mature oaks and along a hard path between houses to a road, coming out opposite the West Norfolk Arts Centre. Turn left.

To visit the castle when it is open, continue over a crossroads and up a small lane, with the high banks of the castle on the right, and turn right into the castle car park and right again to the ticket office. Having explored the castle, leave by continuing along the broad path leading to the village.

To miss out the castle turn right at the crossroads mentioned earlier and walk past a plant centre nestling in the lee of a magnificent old barn. Follow the road as it bends right and reaches another crossroads. Turn right back to the pub.

Places of interest nearby

The *Castle*, a huge 12th century hall keep, one of the grandest in Norfolk, stands in a large complex of earthworks, banks and ditches. Built by William d'Albini, it has had connections with a series of illustrious people including Queen Isabella and the Black Prince. Henry VIII gave it to the Duke of Norfolk, whose descendants still own it. It is in the care of English Heritage and is open daily, except Mondays in winter. Telephone: 01553 631330. Turn left out of the pub to see the *Hospital of the Most Holy and Undivided Trinity*, a lovely 17th century almshouse. The chapel, dining hall and treasury with original Jacobean panelling, furniture and ancient treasury chest are open to the public at certain times or by appointment. For additional walking follow the lovely path to *Wootton Carr* and *Ling Common* through beautiful brackeny woods. The town of *King's Lynn* offers a wealth of beautiful old buildings and some interesting museums. The King's Lynn Festival is held in July. *Wolferton Station Museum* and *Sandringham House* are only a few miles away.

8 Reepham
The Old Brewery House

The Market Place is a lovely square of old houses and shops, in the centre of Reepham. In one corner stands this graceful pub/hotel (20 bedrooms) with its interesting sundial on the front elevation. Until comparatively recently it was a dwelling house associated with the brewery behind, now converted into the hotel's banqueting hall and sports centre. To reach the dark womb-like bar you walk through the panelled hallway with its curving stair rail. There are various pleasant corners off the bar where you can take your drink or meal and a separate panelled room with old photos on the walls. Beyond the bar is the Garden Room, which overlooks a pleasant area with a pond and is used as a games or small function room. Alternatively, meals can be taken in the pretty restaurant overlooking a little railinged garden with outside tables and the Market Place beyond.

The menu is fairly standard but comprehensive and the food is well cooked. Among the snacks you will find stuffed pitta as well as the usual sandwiches and ploughman's. There is a children's menu with six choices and vegetarians are well catered for with such things as mushroom ricarde in a herb and cream sauce. A board offers different specials each day and there is a roast on Sundays. The real ales are

41

excellent and include the local brew, the award winning Reepham Rapier. There is a guest each week (Fuggles for example) as well as Adnams Bitter and Abbot Ale. Murphy's stout and Flowers bitter are on draught as well as Heineken and Stella Artois lagers and Max dry cider. The bar is open virtually all day as it is part of a hotel and meals are served from 12 noon to 2 pm and from 7 pm to 9 pm.

Telephone: 01603 870881.

How to get there: Reepham (9 miles north-west of Norwich) is on the B1145, which leaves the A1067 halfway between Fakenham and Norwich.

Parking: The hotel has parking at the rear and there is limited parking in the square outside. Fisher's Alley nearby leads from a free car park off the main road.

Length of the walk: 3½ miles. Extended walks can be taken along Marriott's Way which goes through Reepham. OS Landranger map 133 North East Norfolk (inn GR 100229).

The architectural pleasures of an interesting old market town and the joys of the pastoral countryside around are combined in this walk, which includes a section along a disused railway line, part of Marriott's Way.

The Walk

Turn left when leaving the pub and walk from the square down the road which leads to the churchyard. Once there were three churches cheek by jowl here, serving three parishes. Now only two still stand and the third is marked by a remnant of old wall. The village sign here depicts three sisters who (it is rumoured) fought with each other so much that each decided to found a separate church to spite the others! Go through the gateway into the churchyard and walk past St Michael's, used as a meeting hall linked to the parish church of St Mary. Continue on and when you leave the churchyard bear left down Church Street to reach the main road, passing the Gothic Old Rectory on the right.

Turn right along the main Norwich Road. Everywhere you look are interesting old houses and alleys. Ignore the turning into Bircham Road on the left. Pass decorative St Mary's School on the right. Shortly after this, turn to the left up an alley leading between hedges and trees. On reaching a road, turn right then left up a lane called The Moor. Ignore the turn to the right leading to Reepham Moor and continue on along the road (now Orchard Road) through housing. The lane narrows and becomes more rural.

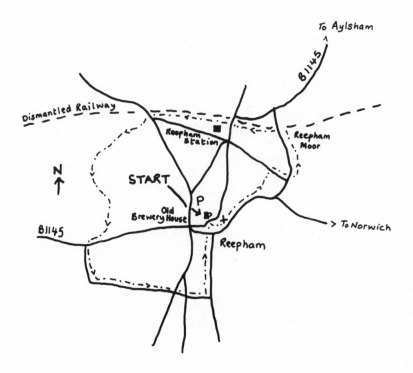

Just before a railway bridge over the lane turn left up a stepped path which leads to the old railway line. Turn left along this (Marriott's Way). Cawston is signposted in the other direction. The line is now just a sandy path here leading between the outlying houses of Reepham towards wooden gates. Go through these and cross over the B1145 Bawdeswell to Aylsham road and go in the direction of Salle, heading for a railway bridge. Go under this, through wooden gates, and continue on past the former railway station – a good coffee stop where, in good weather, tables are set out on the platform. Eventually you reach an embankment from which you can look down through trees to the fields on either side.

Come to a bridge, where a large sign explains the Marriott's Way. This is a 21 mile route for walkers, cyclists or horseriders along old railway lines and is named after William Marriott, who was chief engineer and manager of the Midland and Great Northern Railway for 41 years. Follow steps down the bank on the right, cross a stile at the bottom, turn right and go under the bridge. Beyond the bridge the

Reepham Station Garden.

lane forks. Take the right fork for a short distance and then turn right along a broad, green track, signposted 'Marriott's Way'. Follow the bends of this track (Catchback Lane) through fields. Ignore the footpath which leads through a gate to the right. Continue on until the path reaches a road.

Turn right and walk for a short distance along this road. Opposite a row of brick cottages on the corner, take a left turn off the road down Broomhill Lane, passing a 'No Through Road' sign (arrow marker post). Walk towards a red-brick house. Bear left here onto a green lane and continue on. The Marriott's Way link goes to the right by a school playing field, but this walk continues straight on, heading back towards Reepham. Follow along the edge of a sports field, then come onto a broad swathe of grass near a school. Walk down the road here to a junction, crossing over to walk down Rudd's Lane. This leads to another road junction. Cross and continue ahead along Whitwell Street. Go past a white cottage and turn left down narrow, metalled Bar Lane, where Whitwell Street swings to the right. Keep on ahead, following old walls and ignoring side paths. The path comes out onto a road under an arch. Turn left along Black Street, then turn right through railings along Pudding Pie Alley and, passing public conveniences on the right, come out into the Market Place.

Places of interest nearby

Reepham Station has been filled with an interesting collection of nostalgic bygones, many of interest to children, including a grocer's shop with original mahogany counter and fittings. The tiny cinema with seats from old coaches shows films with Norfolk interest. There is a pretty platform garden with large paving boards for games and bicycles can be hired. Telephone: 01603 871870. *Marriott's Way* can be extended at either end by joining the Bure Valley Walk or the Norwich Riverside Walk. There is also a link to the 56 mile Weavers Way. Leaflets are available from County Hall, Norwich. A few miles away at Great Witchingham is the *Norfolk Wildlife Centre and Country Park* which has a large collection of European and British wildlife in 40 acres of parkland. Telephone: 01603 872274.

Hickling
The Pleasure Boat

Originally this pub was a cottage inn servicing the great wherries which used to ply up and down the broads and through the cuts. There is now a large extension with picture windows overlooking a grassy area and tables for alfresco eating and the wide expanse of Hickling Broad beyond. A cut, with an explanatory board about the broad at one end, provides ample room for boats to moor for the pub.

Everyone is welcome, whether it is families off the boats or people who are just having a day out. The long main bar opens at one end onto a games room with pool and darts. At the other end the restaurant extension, with its cheery blue checked tablecloths, provides plenty of eating room away from the bar area. The menu varies according to the season, with a much bigger selection in summer. Children have their own part of the menu and there is a very popular Sunday lunch, which includes a choice of starter, roast beef, roast pork or scampi as a main course, and a pudding or cheese to finish. Vegetarian food is on offer. There is also a snack menu which offers four choices of jacket potato, five of burger, sandwiches and ploughman's. Out of season the pub keeps normal hours but in the summer it stays open all day, providing morning coffee and tea in the afternoon if required. The range of real ales includes Webster's, Courage Directors, Wadworth 6X, Marston's Pedigree and Morland Old Speckled Hen. On draught are a Dark Mild, Guinness, Woodpecker and Strongbow cider and Foster's and Holsten lager. A choice of three red house wines, three white and a sparkling is offered.

Telephone: 01692 598211.

How to get there: Hickling is signposted from the A149 road between Stalham and Potter Heigham. It consists of the three hamlets of Hickling, Hickling Green and Hickling Heath and the Pleasure Boat is at Hickling Heath, right by the Broad.

Parking: The pub has a very large car park with toilets and showers at one end. There is also parking at the Norfolk Wildlife Trust's visitor centre.

Length of the walk: About 3½ miles. OS Landranger map 134 Norwich and the Broads (inn GR 409225).

This is a walk of waving reed beds and thatched boathouses and barns, of wide expanses of water thronged with birdlife, of mysterious creeks and hidden ditches, of

Lookout at Hickling Nature Reserve.

47

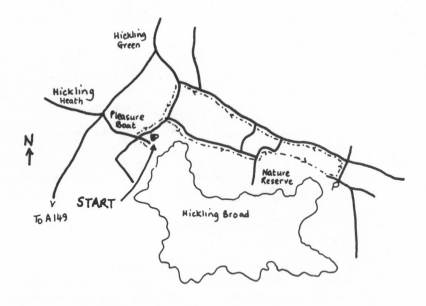

fields and copses and spinneys, of boats and sails — in essence the distillation of broadland. In addition, you can turn off into the Hickling Broad Nature Reserve and immerse yourself in the wildlife and plantlife of this very special area by following the tracks, many of them boarded, through the reserve — a memorable experience at any time of the year.

The Walk

Turn right out of the pub and walk down the approach road next to the car park. At the junction with the main road turn right and follow the road past densely moored boats and Hickling Parish Staithe, bearing right to curve alongside reed beds. Over the fields on the left can be seen a sail-less windmill.

Turn right down Hill Common past large houses on the left and attractive clumps of thatched boathouses edging the broad on the right. Carry straight on along this pretty lane, passing a bungalow on the left. A notice says 'Willow Farm only' but there is a footpath arrow on a post on the left so continue on ahead. Go on into a farmyard with buildings on the left. Bear left, passing a farmhouse on the left, then bear right off the track before it reaches intensive feeding buildings on the left, passing a barn on the right. It can be very muddy along here. The footpath signpost may not be obvious. Follow a hedge on the right, and then the track continues on ahead over a rather overgrown

48

grassy area with a ditch on the right. Walk towards an old oak tree with waymarking on a post to the left here. Cross the bridge and continue across a grassy area planted with young trees, keeping to the right and following the signs towards another bridge by an oak tree. Cross this and go straight ahead across the corner of the field here onto a grassy path along the field edge (arrow pointing back). Continue ahead along a ditch on the right with bushes and trees beyond – an excellent area for wild flowers.

Towards the end of this field look out for a board bridge which leads right into the nature reserve. Follow the path through trees and undergrowth onto a more solid wide path. Continue ahead past a shed on the right and a cottage on the left. Come out onto a lane, with a wooden signpost pointing back. On the right is the reserve's visitor centre.

To extend the walk, follow a boardwalk to a thatched observation hut and continue on to a thatched house on the right, where by turning left over a bridge you can follow a drive right back to the centre. There are alternative walks through the reserve. Trail leaflets are obtainable from the visitor centre or there is an information board.

If you are not visiting the reserve, turn left up the lane, passing the cottage on the left. At the next crossroads, signposted back to the reserve, turn left and continue on down this lane without turning off, passing scattered houses and a bungalow as well as entrances to two farms on the left. There are wide views over fields and woods to Hickling church, over on the right. As you pass through the houses of Hickling Green, ignore turnings to the right and eventually, at a road junction, turn left down Ouse Lane (with views of the windmill). Pass Hill Common, the road taken earlier, and retrace your steps along the road back to the pub.

Places of interest nearby

Hickling Broad has international status under the Ramscar Convention and is a National Nature Reserve of premier importance for wildlife. Boats for a 2½ hour water trail start from the pub. Telephone: 01692 61276. *Sutton Windmill and Broads Museum* is not far away at Stalham. Telephone: 01692 581195.

⑩ Castle Acre
The Ostrich

This three-storey, 16th century coaching inn with its carriage archway forms part of the street scene on one side of Stocks Green in the centre of Castle Acre. The front door opens into a large bar on two levels, each section with its own inglenook fireplace and in really cold weather a help yourself cauldron of soup hangs over the fire. The serving bar rests on large beer barrels. The beamed main bar decorated with old photographs leads into the Top Room, which used to be an old kitchen and pantry and which has now been opened up to the rafters, providing an airy and spacious room of great character. It is useful for families as it is adjacent to the pleasant walled garden, which has tables, an aviary, a dovecote and the added attraction of a herb garden. There is a function room which caters for 50 people, and rooms for bed and breakfast.

The landlord has built up an excellent reputation for his food and has in fact won prizes for his Royal Ostrich Double Decker, which is a brown bread sandwich filled with crab and smoked salmon. Specialities, such as pork and venison pie or beef, aubergine and pasta pie, change every day and new dishes are being developed all the time. The special vegetarian menu offers a delicious spinach and peanut pie. The snack menu includes six varieties of ploughman's, including fisherman's with cockles and mussels. The junior menu has six choices, too, and the sweets are delicious, for example baclava and rum baba. Food is served from 12 noon to 2 pm and from 7.15 pm to 10.30 pm on Monday to Saturday, with the kitchen closing a little earlier on Sunday. The beers are exceptionally well kept and include Abbot and Greene King IPA and Dark Mild. Normal pub hours operate.

Telephone: 01760 755398.

How to get there: Castle Acre is just off the A1065 road from Fakenham 4 miles north of Swaffham. Follow signs to the priory, which is a few hundred yards west of Stocks Green and the Ostrich.

Parking: There is a car park at the rear of the pub through the archway.

Length of the walk: 3 miles (with short cuts for wheelchairs and pushchairs). OS Landranger map 132 North West Norfolk (inn GR 816151).

The views from this walk are exceptionally attractive. By following tiny lanes, including part of Peddars Way, out into the countryside and fording the river Nar at a very pretty spot, the wonderful ruins of the priory with its Tudor gatehouse can be seen from several different angles, sometimes framed with overhanging boughs. As it is mostly on roads this walk would be suitable for wheelchairs and pushchairs, though there are one or two muddy corners when approaching the hamlet of South Acre. As you circle back towards Castle Acre, the massive mound and earthworks come into view. The walk explores the castle remains, from which there are magnificent views over the surrounding countryside, before returning through the narrow bailey gate to the domestic architecture of attractive Stocks Green, with its pubs, restaurants, tearooms and shops, all looking onto the green and its row of lovely old lime trees.

The Walk

Turn right out of the pub, down the lane beyond the green, passing the interesting church of St James the Great. Take the next small lane (South Acre Road) to the left by 15th century Priory Lodge – possibly once a chapel (note the splendid chequered stone and flint work) – and follow it, passing Chimney Street on the left, then another little lane. Both these lanes are suitable for short cuts. This is now part of the Peddars Way, which is a long distance walk from Knettishall Heath, near Thetford, to Holme-next-the-Sea, near Hunstanton. It is an ancient route, utilised by the Romans as a military road.

The ruins of the priory can be seen on the right behind the hedge.

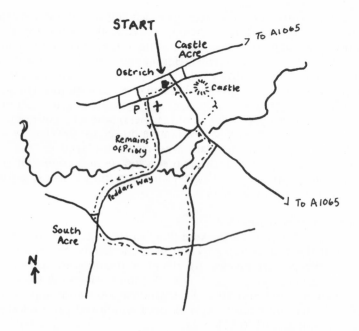

Not everyone heeds the sign 'Ford Unsuitable for Motors' – I have certainly seen a car stuck in the water! The lane passes through water meadows and then goes alongside the river on the left, with a footbridge by the ford. The river bears off right through the meadows and the lane continues on uphill. Bear left round a muddy corner by farm barns and continue on past a red-brick house on the left. A lane comes in from the right at a wooded corner and shortly after this where a bigger road comes in from the right there is a wooden marker saying 'Long Distance Path'.

Go onto the main road for a step or two and then bear immediately left down another small lane, which gives exciting views over the scene of fields and woodland surrounding Castle Acre, with its beautiful priory at one end and its high castle mound and walls at the other. The lane meanders downhill between meadows and fields. At a crossroads turn left onto a wider road with a width limit sign. At a junction of roads bear left along the more main road, which crosses over the river and bears round to the right. Blind Lane, leading to Chimney Street, comes in from the right. Pass old cottages on the right. Wheelchairs and pushchairs should continue up Bailey Street.

To walk on the castle remains, turn right up Cuckstool Street and onto a path to the left of a metal gate, leading to a bungalow, then climb steeply to the left up to the impressive castle earthworks. Cross a flattish area and go over a bridge leading to the remains of the main keep. The castle, now an English Heritage property, was based on a Norman manor house. After exploring the ruins, take the path to the right of the bridge as you come back over it, passing through some more ruins and over a ditch and out through wooden gates. Continue ahead down the alley, passing an old chapel on the left. Turn right up Bailey Street, passing the Old Red Lion (a hostel) on the right, which has a large map of the Peddars Way route displayed on the wall outside. Go through the 13th century gateway and come out onto Stocks Green, opposite the Albert Victor pub from where it is just a step or two back to the Ostrich.

Places of interest nearby

The *Cluniac Priory* at Castle Acre (English Heritage) was founded at the end of the 11th century by the Warenne family. Set in a lovely valley sweeping down towards the river Nar, the ruins are approached through a splendid Tudor gatehouse. The impressive west front with its Norman entrance and great west window still stands and next to it are a Norman undercroft with an oriel windowed prior's lodging above. Telephone: 01760 755394.

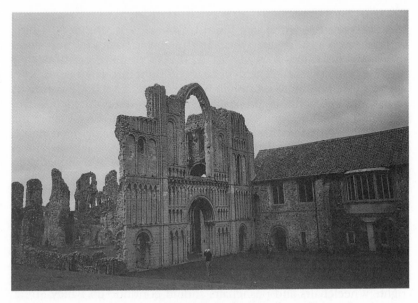

Castle Acre Priory.

⑪ Gressenhall
The Swan

On the green at Gressenhall stands this neat, white-painted pub with black eyebrows over the windows and a welcoming bench outside. Inside there is a large bar with darts and a dining area with a woodburning stove and shelves of cottagey china. Round the corner is a further dining area, suitable for children as french windows lead into an enclosed garden. Unusually for a pub, the family dog is given a warm welcome.

The food is all home-made and a choice of several vegetables is offered. The menu is written up on a board and includes such things as pork steak in a cream cheese and mushroom sauce or vegetable beanfeast chilli. Small portions can be given on request and old fashioned puds are available. On Thursdays there is a senior citizens lunch at a set price and a roast is available on Sundays. Greene King IPA and Abbot are the real ales, though sometimes this changes and additional guest beers are offered. On draught are Tetley Bitter, Labatt's and Carlsberg Export lagers and Dry Blackthorn cider. The pub keeps normal opening hours and food is served from 12 noon to 2 pm and from 7 pm to 9 pm, except on Mondays when no food is available.

Telephone: 01632 860340.

How to get there: Gressenhall is north-west of East Dereham and is signposted off the B1146 road, south of Brisley.

Parking: There is parking in front of the pub, on the green or at the Rural Life museum.

Length of the walk: 4½ miles. OS Landranger map 132 North West Norfolk (inn GR 964166).

The tiny lanes leading from Gressenhall run through a wet landscape of marsh and carr woodland — an excellent habitat for birds, herons being particularly numerous. At the centre of the walk is a large lake area and occasional tantalising views of this appear through the trees. An unusual feature of the latter part of the walk is that it goes through acres of orchards and soft fruit fields — a wonderful sight and scent in spring and again at fruiting time. After these bosky groves it is quite a shock to see the huge imposing building of the former Gressenhall workhouse, home to the Rural Life museum, looming up out of its surrounding farmland.

The Walk

Turn right out of the pub and walk alongside the pretty green on the left, past the pond shaded by two weeping willow trees. Continue on down the lane ahead (Bridge Street). Cross the road bridge over a little stream and at a road junction keep on ahead along the lane signposted to Dereham. The lane to the right, signposted to Longham, offers a longer loop, passing the church, which can be seen across the fields on the right.

Pass Rectory Farm and then a lovely brick and flint barn on the left. Soon after Rectory Cottages and a red-brick house, there is a good view through a gateway of the water, marsh and carr woodland, a most interesting-looking area full of birdlife. The pretty, leafy lane passes the entrance to the Rectory on the right and then some cottages on the left. Ignore the turn on the right leading to Longham and continue on along the Dereham road, bearing left past some more cottages. The lane becomes leafy again and passes through fields, crossing another small road bridge over a stream. The countryside dotted with the odd dwelling is rough, swampy carr here, with gorse and bracken and lots of lovely mature trees.

Shortly before a house which stands up on the left take a wide, stony track to the left, signposted to Drift Farm. At the driveway to Drift Farm, which says 'Private No Entry', follow a narrow green lane to the right, which wends its way through overhanging trees. The path climbs gently and passes along the edge of a field of soft fruit on the left. Continue on along the edge of another two fields of soft fruit, and then an apple orchard. At a crossing of tracks by two large oak trees

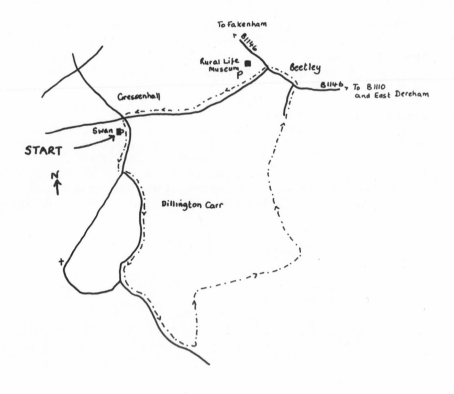

(arrow signpost on the right), turn left at a sign warning that dogs should be kept on leads (red arrow on a board), down a nut and holly hedge on the left. There are more apple orchards over on the right. Eventually there is an opening into the orchard on the left with a notice saying 'Private Property Keep Out'. Step through the hedge here, then continue on ahead, in the same direction as before, along a small metalled road, but with the hedge now on the right. There is the odd red arrow in sight, sometimes pointing backwards. The road does a little wiggle at another red arrow. Continue on through more soft fruit. At the end of a row of poplars on the right there is a crossway. Go ahead onto a grassy path here (another arrow on the back of a board) and walk through trees. Continue on past an opening into a private property on the left. Pass a house with Gothic windows and continue on between more houses and an old open fronted barn on the left to come out onto the main road.

Bear left along the main road for a short distance, passing a house on the left. The river goes under the road. Pass the 'Beetley' sign and turn left, signposted to Gressenhall and Litcham and the 'Museum of Rural Life'. The huge red-brick former workhouse which houses the museum is on the opposite side of the road from Union Farm and its farm walk. Continue along the road towards Gressenhall village green, ignoring all turnings.

Places of interest nearby

The *Norfolk Rural Life Museum* should not be missed. As well as many crafts and exhibits housed in the old workhouse and its associated buildings, there is a working 1920s farm and nature trail. Telephone: 01362 860563. Just on the other side of the B1146 near Gressenhall is *Hoe Rough*, a fine example of unimproved grassland with woodland and mossy heath, belonging to the Norfolk Wildlife Trust.

12 South Walsham
The Ship

The old anchor leaning up against the pub sign is one indication of the nautical connections of this 17th century coaching inn. The lounge door with its mirrored porthole leads into a small beamed bar, simply furnished with etchings and paintings of ships on the wall, an oar along the bar and various bits of ship's block and tackle on display. Through a beamed arch and up two steps is the intimate restaurant area and its mirror decorated with a large ship in coloured glass. There is talk of a priest's hole and tunnel leading from the pub to the church over the road. To the left of the front door is a games bar with seats in the curve of the bay window and a wintertime open fire. Bordering the car park at the back is a covered way leading to a special children's room containing toys, and there are tables and a swing and a slide in the fenced garden area, next to an enclosure for a family of pet goats. There are also a few tables on a terrace in front of the cream-painted building, which is decorated with colourful tubs and hanging baskets in summer.

The Ship is a freehouse, serving John Smith's, Adnams Bitter and Woodforde's Wherry real ales, with Simmond's Bitter, Courage Dark Mild and Beamish on draught. Foster's and Holsten Export are the lagers, with Red Rock cider. There is a small but interesting choice of wines by the glass. The excellent food is mostly home-made and among more traditional dishes are some very different ideas, such as Japanese-style prawns with a spicy dip, or the Ship special of turkey in a mild curry sauce. Ten vegetables cooked in a pea and lentil sauce with garlic, herbs and spices and served with a hot crusty loaf is a delicious mouthful for vegetarians! Special dishes are written up on a blackboard. On Thursday, Friday and Saturday evenings there is a set gourmet meal which must be pre-booked and to which you can bring your own bottle of wine. The pub keeps normal opening hours on weekdays and Sundays but is open all day on Saturdays in summer and winter.

Telephone: 01603 270553.

How to get there: South Walsham is on the B1140 between Acle and Norwich. The Ship is on the main street, almost opposite the church.

Parking: There is parking at the Ship or at South Walsham Broad.

Length of the walk: About 3½ miles, with opportunities for longer walks along Fleet Dyke and in Upton Fen. OS Landranger map 134 Norwich and the Broads (inn GR 364132).

This is a gentle ramble through typical broadland scenery – fields and woods, water, marsh and fen. The views across the broad are delightful and the unspoilt wildlife of Upton Fen is a real treat.

The Walk

Turn right out of the pub and walk along the main street, passing the churchyard on the left. There are two parish churches, the remains of St Lawrence's and 14th/15th century St Mary's. Over the road are The Old Rectory and The Old Vicarage next to each other! Pass a lovely barn on the corner after the church then South Walsham Hall, now a country club and restaurant. Turn left down School Lane, signposted to Upton, pass a house on the left then the car park of the Fairhaven Trust.

Not long after the school a signposted footpath goes to the left through the middle of a field. The path comes out into a small lane. Continue ahead, with a house and a thatched barn on the right. Come to cottages edging the broad and carr woodland on the right. Bear left at the corner along an unmade up track, ignoring the track which goes straight ahead. Go through scattered housing, with views of the broad on the left. This is Kingfisher Lane which comes out at a junction of lanes and a small car park. Turn left to go along Fleet Lane which leads

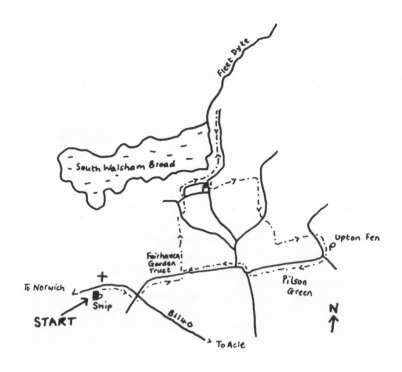

to the staithe. The lane bears left, passing a summer shop and boatyards. You can hire boats and day launches from here and there are toilets on the right. You can continue on for as long as you like along this path, which carries on along the Fleet Dyke (arrow marker as you come through by a fence).

To continue the walk, return down Fleet Lane and bear left at the junction of lanes then almost immediately turn left along a signposted footpath, going alongside gardens on the left and a field on the right. Go through the hedgerow at the end of gardens where there is a green arrow signpost and continue on ahead on the other side of the hedge, which is now on the right. At a muddy lane turn right, passing thatched Townhouse Farm on the right. Before the lane bends to the right there is a footpath signpost on the right, pointing across the lane into a field. Bear left through metal gates and follow round the edge of the field. Continue to the end of the hedge on the left and then go on a little way along a baulk to a yellow arrow marker near a tree. Turn left here across the field towards red-brick cottages ahead and come out into a lane (signpost pointing back).

Turn right and immediately on the left is a car park for Upton Fen. The nature reserve (Norfolk Wildlife Trust) is spring fed and thus of importance for its high water quality which encourages abundant insect and plant life, including the marsh helleborine and southern marsh orchid. A nature trail leads past turf ponds with unique wildlife and continues on to one of the best views in broadland. There is an explanatory board in the car park.

For the main walk, continue along the lane, passing Fen House on the left. A track goes off on the left to houses, but immediately after this is a road junction. Take the right turn, signposted to South Walsham, passing the housing of Pilson Green on the right. Continue on past a right turn into an estate to a road junction. Turn right at the junction and walk to the right down School Lane. Bear left round the corner and continue on, ignoring Broad Lane on the right. Pass a large pond on the right, then Manor Farm on the left. Pass the path through the field on the right, which was taken on the outward journey, and retrace your steps through the village back to the pub.

Places of interest nearby

Fairhaven Garden Trust is a beautiful woodland and water garden overlooking inner South Walsham Broad. A vintage river boat runs trips on the broads. Telephone: 01603 270449. *Ranworth Broad Nature Reserve* (Norfolk Wildlife Trust) is only a couple of miles away and has a floating conservation and information centre as well as a nature trail.

13 Filby
The Fox and Hounds

This is a friendly and unpretentious village local with a modest menu of typical pub food, for example a sea food platter with salad and chips. There is also a children's menu, or small portions can be served. The landlady is happy to cook at any reasonable time and the pub is open all day in summer, which is a real help to hungry walkers. Flowers IPA is the real ale, and Labatt's, Stella Artois and Carlsberg lagers are on offer, as well as Murphy's, Guinness, Ind Coope Dark Mild and Red Rock cider.

At the back of the red-brick pub is a garden with tables and children's play things, alongside guinea pigs and rabbits in very smart designer houses. The two bars are cheerfully decorated in warm reds, brightened with swags and baskets of luxuriant artificial flowers. Horse brasses gleam and stuffed animals and birds peer down from shelves. One bar, where children are welcome, has darts, a pool table and a large TV. In summer real flowers tumble from the tubs and hanging baskets outside.

Telephone: 01493 369255.

How to get there: The village of Filby straddles the A1064 road a few miles west of Caister. The Fox and Hounds is a little way up the turning signposted to Thrigby.

Parking: There is plenty of parking at the back of the pub or by the A1064 bridge near the broads, just west of the village.

Length of the walk: About 3 miles (or a shorter route for wheelchairs and pushchairs). OS Landranger map 134 Norwich and the Broads (inn GR 465132).

The route of this walk passes through the pretty village of Filby to the hamlet of Thrigby, where often a tiger belonging to Thrigby Hall Wildlife Gardens can be seen pacing behind bars near the road. The foreign calls of exotic birds ring out through the pastoral Norfolk scenery and sometimes escaped cranes feed in the fields. The walk reaches a splendid old postmill (one of only two in Norfolk) and then turns back downhill towards Filby church. There are lovely wide views of broadland scenery. A shorter loop of the village, turning off the lane near the pub, is suitable for wheelchairs and pushchairs.

The broads near Filby.

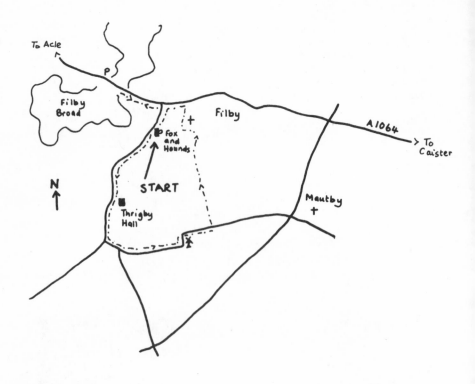

The Walk

Turn left out of the pub and continue up through houses past the delimit sign, bearing left round the corner. Continue following the curves of the road with its farmland views, then pass Hall Farm and a pretty thatched gatehouse to The Hall on the left. Soon after the church of St Mary is the entrance drive to the wildlife gardens, with good views of the hall and its ponds, enclosures and aviaries.

Turn left at the next road junction, signposted to Runham and Mautby. At another road junction bear left in the direction of Mautby. Pass a little spinney on the left and continue on along this road, lined with a band of woodland on the right, towards an old windmill which dates from the 1790s. There are amazing views over the countryside from here. A board shows the routes of the Filby Parish Walks and gives information about Thrigby postmill.

A footpath is signposted to the left along the edge of fields, which can be used as a slightly shorter cut to return to Filby.

For the full walk continue on along the road from the mill, passing Mill Cottage on the right. You can see the tiny church of St Peter and

St Paul at Mautby, where Margaret Paston (co-author of the *Paston Letters*) was buried, from here and way over on the right lie Halvergate Marshes and the sea.

Turn left where a bridleway crosses the road, marked by a wooden signpost. Walk down a muddy and rutted track along the edge of the field with a row of mature trees on the right. The trees and the hedgerow end but the bridleway goes straight ahead towards Filby church (arrow marker on post) through the middle of a wide field. In the distance, in the trees beyond the church, are glimpses of the white sails of a wind farm. At a farmyard with a barn on the right the path continues straight on to the church but can be very muddy.

Go ahead to a lane, ignoring a path which goes to the right. Pass the churchyard on the left and at the red-brick and cobbled wall of the church turn left into the churchyard through a metal kissing gate (footpath signpost) and continue along the church wall. Turn right through a gap in the wall and walk past the church on the right or for a short cut turn left along the public footpath which goes through a gate and eventually reaches the lane near the Fox and Hounds. Visit Filby All Saints church to see the restored paintings on the medieval screen – the finest in Norfolk.

Continue on down the path from the church through gates and out to a lane, which soon reaches the main road. Turn left here and walk along the pavement, passing the thatched village club and the playing fields on the right. The walk goes back to the pub to the left up the next lane, but it is worth carrying on along the main road for a short distance to the bridge where there are lovely views over the broads (Ormesby Little Broad and Filby Broad) on either side. A board in the car park by the bridge gives information about other walks in the area. There is a boardwalk leading to a hide.

Places of interest nearby

Thrigby Hall Wildlife Gardens have a wide selection of Asian mammals, birds and reptiles in the landscaped grounds of a country mansion. Telephone: 01493 369477. A mile or so from Filby is *Fleggburgh Bygone Heritage Village* which is a re-creation of a 19th century village, complete with steam road engines and old cars. Telephone: 01493 369770. Further down the A1064 is *Caister*, with its Roman town and the car collection ranging from 1893 to the present day, housed in a half-ruined 15th century castle at West Caister.

14 Denver
The Bell Inn

This pleasant looking carr stone pub, hung with flowering baskets in summer, offers a warm welcome to locals and visitors alike. The large bar area is covered with a red fitted carpet patterned with small bells and has comfortable red velvet benches. There is always an open fire in winter. Cups and trophies decorate every ledge, spoils of the many football, darts, pool, dominoes and crib teams run by the pub. Steps lead down to a restaurant, dominated by a mural of Denver Mill, and a large games room, which also doubles as a function room for private parties. Outside steps also go from the main bar into the well organised garden where, as well as a pretty pool with fish and an aviary, there is a children's play area which includes a sandpit. Attractive tubs add to the cheerful scene.

The pub serves Boddingtons Mild and Bitter as well as Greene King IPA and Webster's Cask. Also on draught are Carlsberg, Muller and Kronenbourg lagers, Guinness and Dry Blackthorn cider. Traditional pub food, often home-cooked by the landlady herself, is offered and a children's menu is also available. There is a choice of three different curries (beef, chicken or vegetable) and roast beef is served on Sunday lunchtimes, followed by home-made apple and fruit pies. Food can be

The windmill at Denver.

ordered from 12 noon to 2 pm and from 7 pm to 10 pm every day except Mondays, although on Sunday evenings the kitchen shuts half an hour earlier. Normal pub opening times are kept.

Telephone: 01366 382173.

How to get there: Denver is 2 miles south of Downham Market and is just off the A10. The Bell stands on a junction of three roads in the centre of the village, opposite the church.

Parking: There is parking at the pub and limited parking by the mill. A large riverside car park can be found at Denver Sluice, a mile from the village.

Length of the walk: 2½ miles (with optional extensions to the mill and Denver Sluice or a short cut for wheelchairs and pushchairs). OS Landranger map 143 Ely, Wisbech (inn GR 614015).

Denver is an attractive village, noted for its carr stone houses and beautiful church and graveyard. The walk follows pretty tracks to attractive tree-strewn Whin Common, to the east of the village. A longer stroll will take the walker to the restored mill standing on the edge of marshy fields and further on to the interesting complex of waterways at Denver Sluice, where raised banks offer superb views of the surrounding countryside and the boat and birdlife of the rivers.

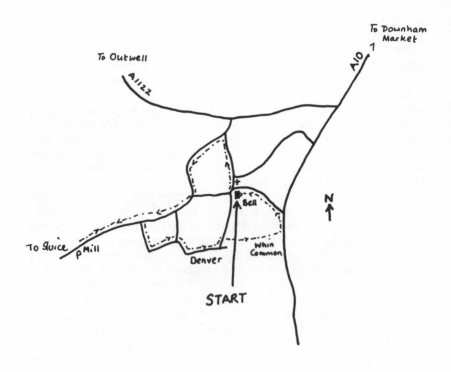

The Walk

Leave the pub by the front entrance, cross over Sluice Road and take Downham Road, which bears right, round the church, passing a cul-de-sac and the Old Rectory on the right and the village shop on the left. Continue on along the road past buildings made from the local deep brown carr stone, either built up in great chunks like the church or piled up like small tiles as in the shop. The road soon passes playing fields on the right.

Turn left down Sandy Lane, passing the graveyard on the left. The broad, stony lane eventually bears left to more houses. Continue on to where the track becomes a road. Come out at a T-junction by a little green and turn right along the road leading to Denver Sluice. Pass a large green area leading to old College Farm on the left and continue down the road to the mill on the left. A mile further on is Denver Sluice. There is a footpath to the left through a meadow beyond the mill, then left again to walk behind the mill. If this is obstructed, return up the road, looking out for Brady Close on the right. For pushchairs and wheelchairs go straight back to the pub.

To continue the walk, turn right over wooden bars up a narrow signposted track beside a house called Mulberry Tree, just past Brady Close. Cross a green area in the middle of an estate and continue up a narrow, fenced path to the left of some conifers, passing between dwellings to emerge at a junction of broad tracks with open country ahead. Ignore the track going ahead and turn left along the track which borders the gardens of houses and then meadows on the left. At a T-junction of broad tracks turn right. At the next junction of tracks bear left, ignoring the track which goes on ahead. Pass between houses to a small lane and bear right.

Follow a little path onto the common and just past a pretty old brick and carr stone cottage a road veers away on the right. Cross a little bridge and continue following the path. Come onto a mown area and bear left, passing the garden of a pretty cottage along a wide, mown track leading to a stile. Cross this and continue on across Whin Common, with a hedge of brambles and trees on the left. The path is faint but keep generally towards the left-hand boundary of this bumpy, tree-dotted area. Come out under an old oak tree across a signposted stile onto the verge of the main road.

Walk with care to the left for a short way, then turn left down the tree-lined B1507, signposted to Denver. Pass a water garden and a house on the left and continue on, following the lovely old carr stone wall and eventually coming back into Denver village.

Places of interest nearby

Denver Tower Mill, one of the tallest in Norfolk, was built in 1835 and ceased functioning in 1969. Having undergone extensive repairs, it is administered by the Norfolk Mills and Pumps Trust and is open from April to September on Wednesday, Saturday and bank holidays from 10 am to 4 pm. *Denver Sluice* is the key to understanding the complexities of the management and drainage of the Fens. It is the meeting point of a network of waterways both natural and man-made where a system of sluices controls the flow of water and allows navigation from Peterborough to Ely, Bedford and Cambridge. It has a long history which is explained (together with the engineering) on a board at the sluice. Boats can be hired here for exploring the waterways.

⑮ Oxborough
The Bedingfeld Arms

The Bedingfeld Arms stands in a lovely rural setting near the charming half-ruined church of St John the Evangelist, not far from the old red-brick walls of Oxburgh Hall. The three-storey, white-painted pub has plenty of tables, for use on a warm day, in a large garden shaded by mature trees, with swings and a climbing frame to amuse children. The interior of the pub is fairly casual and consists of a large carpeted bar with a pool table and darts at one side. The walls here are covered with interesting old photographs, while next door in the restaurant are *Hamlet* etchings.

The food is all freshly prepared and there is an excellent vegetarian menu, which includes Spanish vegetable tortilla (a kind of omelette) and Cambridgeshire pie (wheatmeal crust filled with cauliflower, sweetcorn, beans and onions in Stilton sauce). There is a normal bar menu, an à la carte menu at lunchtimes and Thursday to Sunday evenings, and roasts are served on Sunday and bank holiday lunchtimes. There are daily specials such as steak and ale pie or chilli and rice with tortilla chips, and a range of filled jacket potatoes. Garlic bread is a delicious extra. This freehouse serves Theakston Best Bitter and Old Peculier and Hook Norton Best Bitter, though these are

Oxburgh Hall.

changed round with other real ales. Keg beers include Younger's Mild and Bitter, Gillespie's stout and McEwans and Becks lagers. Strongbow cider is also available on draught.

Telephone: 01366 328300.

How to get there: Oxborough is a few miles north-east of Stoke Ferry and can be reached from the A134 road which runs from Thetford in the direction of King's Lynn. The pub is on a crossroads near the village green and the church.

Parking: There is parking outside the pub, or in the National Trust car park when Oxburgh Hall is open.

Length of the walk: 4½ miles. OS Landranger map 143 Ely, Wisbech (inn GR 745015).

The special attraction of this walk is its wide and lonely landscapes, with a wonderful backdrop of trees on every side. These range from small stands of poplars and conifers to huge mixed woods and individual trees of great variety and interest. The treescape is enhanced by the ancient plantings of the Oxburgh estate and the countryside is typical of Breckland – on parts of the walk there is not a building in sight.

The Walk

Turn right out of the pub and walk down a small road, passing cottages and then the village stores on the left. Continue on into an alleyway leading to houses. Halfway down look carefully for a stile on the right. Cross it and bear left along the back of gardens with chain link fencing and then cross another stile into a field. Near an arrow marker bear left, keeping a field on the right and more gardens and a nice beech hedge on the left. At the end of the hedge there is a green cross track. Cross it and continue on. The track along the edge of the field on the left is quite wide and follows a hedge with young trees in it on the right. The little river Gadder runs through trees some way over on the right. The track kinks to the right and left again, arriving at a fenced field with a stile into it. Cross this and continue along the left-hand boundary of the field. Go over another stile (signposted) next to a metal gate onto a little road.

Turn left up the road past old brick cottages on the right. At a crossroads (Oxborough left and Cockley Cley, with its fascinating museums, right) cross over by a grassy triangle and walk up the wide-verged road ahead. This road goes almost dead straight for about a mile and has lovely views of woods, from which pheasants emerge to scratch on the fields. At last a bend in the road comes into sight. Ignore the farm track which goes off to the right and follow the road as it bends to the left towards farm buildings almost hidden in trees. Just to the right of a lovely old brick flint and clunch building, near the bumpy site of ruined St Mary's church, a wide track goes ahead as the road bends to the right. Follow the arrow-marked track as it veers to the left through farmland. The track eventually passes through mature trees and mixed hedges then, as it comes out into the open, it bears right through fields towards a treed hedgerow bordering lonely Eastmoor Road.

Turn left along the road and then pass cottages on the right. Eventually, the houses of Oxborough come into view. Cross over the first crossroads in the village to arrive at the next crossroads with the 14th century church (well worth a visit for its Bedingfeld Chapel) on the right and the pub on the left. Further on down the road ahead is the Oxburgh Hall car park.

Places of interest nearby

Oxburgh Hall, with its magnificent Tudor gatehouse, is a romantic 15th century rose-brick house which seems to float on its surrounding moat. Its owners, the Bedingfeld family, still live here. It has connections with Mary, Queen of Scots, whose embroidery graces the interesting interior, and has lovely gardens and woodland walks. Telephone: 01366 328258. *Oxborough Woods* (about 2 miles down the

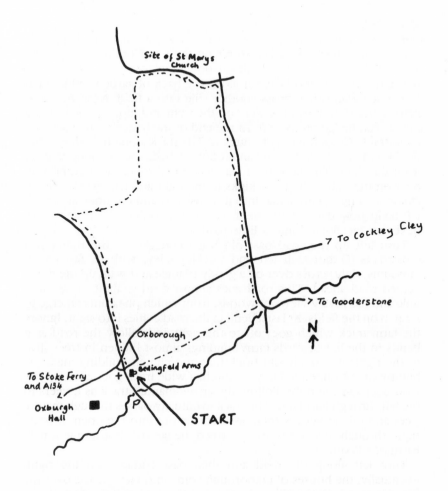

road which leads to the A134) has 90 acres of woodland and riverside walks. Public access on Sundays and bank holidays only, summer months, from 10 am to 5 pm. At nearby *Cockley Cley* is a reconstruction of an Iceni village, believed to be on the riverside site of an original settlement of Queen Boudicca's time. Here also is a museum of East Anglian exhibits, housed in a lovely Elizabethan cottage, while a carriage collection and farming implements are displayed in an old stable block. Telephone: 01760 721339. Nearby is a Saxon church, one of the oldest in the country.

16 **Wymondham**
The Green Dragon

This fascinating late 14th century building is one of the oldest in Wymondham. An ancient carved, bearded head holds up its jettied overhang and the higgledy-piggledy beamed exterior is pierced with old shop (town house) windows. The stout wooden main door takes you almost straight into the Snug Bar where a door in the corner is reputed to lead to a secret tunnel to the abbey – other hidden passages are whispered about. In this bar there is an old settle and a wintertime open fire in a lovely fireplace, the mantelpiece of which is held up by a carved head of Pan. It is laden with bottles, mugs and other domestic or farming knick-knacks. The dining room is cosy, with a rich red carpet, curtains and fringed lampshades. A sampler and intriguing photos cover the walls. There is a small brick fireplace and time-worn beams everywhere – with a venerable 14th century beam running the length of the interior. There is a sheltered garden at the back, with tables under a pergola. The pub does bed and breakfast, some rooms being in the oldest wing.

The food is excellent. The landlord and his wife take a special interest in unusual and often old recipes, and produce prize winning dishes, such as lamb stuffed with spiced crab meat and tart of apple

and quince. There are five different vegetables on offer. Lunchtime and evening have their own menus and 20 or more specials are advertised on blackboards above the bar. The pub serves bar drawn beers. There are three real ales – Greene King IPA, Bass and a guest beer. Carlsberg and Stella Artois lagers are on draught, as is Guinness.
Telephone: 01953 607907.

How to get there: Wymondham is about 8 miles south-west of Norwich and is bypassed by the A11. The Green Dragon is next door to the library in Church Street, just off the bottom of Market Street.

Parking: There is very limited parking at the Green Dragon but Wymondham has several public car parks, the nearest being off Market Street.

Length of the walk: About 2 miles. The whole walk is suitable for wheelchairs or pushchairs. OS Landranger map 144 Thetford and Breckland (inn GR 108016).

This very enjoyable walk makes the most of exploring a small market town full of architectural delights of various periods and diverse materials. Many of its houses were restored or rebuilt after a devastating fire in 1615. The route goes past most of the notable buildings, breaking off at the river Tiffey to meander along its pretty banks, where ducks and cows dabble and drink, for an outstanding view of the great abbey and its associated ruins rising up from the surrounding water meadows.

The Walk

Turn left out of the pub, passing the library in the early 15th century chapel of St Thomas à Becket. It has served many purposes in its time including, housing a guild and a grammar school founded by Elizabeth I. Turn right into Market Street, which is now a mixture of buildings of all ages with the coaching arches of the former Griffin Inn on the right and the White Hart on the left (the latter's Georgian front conceals an old timber-framed building behind). On the right is a large central car park with toilets by the old fire station. Go up to the lovely Market Cross, built in 1617, in Market Place.

Walk up the left-hand street (Bridewell Street with its jettied overhangs), passing the Queen's Head pub on the right. Next door to this is the Manor House, built just after the fire, with an interesting Latin inscription above the door. Carry on to the road junction where facing you is the Bridewell (prison) built in 1785.

Cross to it, then bear right. On the opposite corner of Browick Road is a chapel of 1848, now converted. Bear right at the road junction along Avenue Road to a pleasant green called Fairland, where fairs

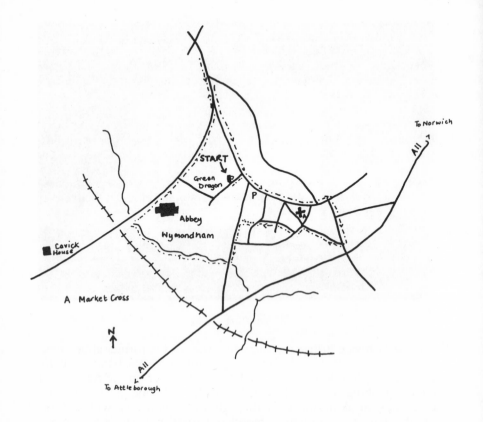

were held following a charter granted by King John. Bear right down
a little slip road past the graveyard of the United Reform church, built
in 1715. Bear right again at the road junction down Fairland Street.
Turn left before reaching the Market Place into a lane called Friarscroft
and then almost immediately turn right into Brewery Lane, a kind of
back service lane which led to the former brewery. The Baptist church
is on the left. Carry on over the junction past a car park on the right.
There is a lovely view of the abbey and the interesting roofscape of
Wymondham from here. Avoid Chandler's Hill on the left and go
down a small path called Chain Entry. This narrow path passes the
timbered wall of an old building and comes out under an arch into
Damgate Street. This old street, with tantalising views of the abbey, is
full of a variety of buildings, some with jettied overhangs, some with
arches. Turn left and walk past the white painted Sun Inn, on the left,
dating from the 1600s, which has an unusual thatched roof behind its
Dutch gable.

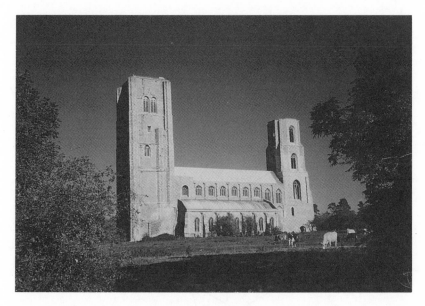

Wymondham Abbey.

Cross Damgate Bridge (recalling the dam for the former abbey mill, over the little river Tiffey and turn right along its bank, walking between modern housing on the left and the river on the right. Soon after a rushing weir, the metalled path ends and a rough track continues on along the river through a common area with a pond on the left. Go through a wooden barrier next to a gate onto Becketswell Road.

For a short diversion to see Cavick House (Queen Anne), turn left here, over the level crossing, and walk for about a mile to find the house on the right.

For the main walk, turn right along Becketswell Road, go over the brick bridge over the river and continue alongside the old brick and cob wall of the abbey. Go through gates leading to the abbey, follow the path out of the churchyard into Church Street and turn left, passing a pleasant brick building which was a Sunday school in 1812. Walk along Vicar Street, at the bottom of which is the war memorial on a junction of roads. Turn left here and walk down Town Green. The ornate Methodist church is on the right and the Feathers pub on the left. Facing you over the road junction is a pleasant curved terrace of 17th century buildings. Bear left and continue down Cock Street to the Cock pub on the left.

Return back up Cock Street, pausing to look down Pople Street on the left, with its rather prim late Victorian terraces. Then go over the traffic island and up Middleton Street, whose houses (such as Beech House on the left and Caius House on the right) have a mainly Georgian aspect. The Priory on the right has an 18th century façade and a fleur de lys crest, indicating its use in the 19th century as the grammar school (founded in 1567 by the Archbishop of Canterbury). Beyond the post office is the Georgian council offices building, behind which is the Wymondham Heritage museum opposite an old coach house. Turn right to the Green Dragon.

Places of interest nearby

Wymondham Heritage Museum in Middleton Street provides an excellent booklet entitled 'A walk around old Wymondham' giving historical details (available also from the library). Telephone: 01953 604650. The *Abbey Church of St Mary and St Thomas of Canterbury*, one of the finest in East Anglia, is the sole surviving section of a once enormous abbey, standing in extensive ruins. It was founded as a priory by William d'Albini in 1107, becoming an abbey in 1448. Guide books can be bought in the shop under the west tower. The railway station houses a collection of railway memorabilia.

Reedham
The Ferry Inn

This freehouse has been run by the same family for a long time. It was originally (in the late 17th century) a marsh farmhouse with a ferry business, serving ales to passengers and wherry boatmen. Now pleasure craft moor up outside for refreshment. Some old deeds concerning the ferry, dated 1773, are framed and displayed on the wall. The main bar is dark and cosy, with a tiled floor and old furniture. The beamed ceiling is hung with agricultural implements and a collection of business cards. Through an arch is another room with ancient pews and settles. From the large, bright front extension there are lovely views across the marshes. Over the lane by the water is a paved patio area, backed with rose covered arches and illuminated by old street lamps, where you can eat, drink and watch the river traffic and birdlife. There are plenty of moorings and a slipway for launching boats. The pub also has showers for boat people and for its camping and caravan site. To one side of the pub is a craft workshop specialising in solid elm furniture.

Several blackboards, hung over the woodburning stove in the bar, advertise delicious food like roast Norfolk chicken with savoury chestnut stuffing or half a roast Norfolk duckling in port wine and plum sauce. All vegetables are freshly cooked to order and the menu is well thought out, with imaginative options for light lunches. There is a separate vegetarian and pudding menu. Real ales are Adnams Bitter and Broadside, Woodforde's Wherry and occasional guest beers. Other beers on draught are Younger Mild and Tartan, Murphy's and Guinness, and Scrumpy Jack cider as well as Carlsberg and Holsten lagers. Norfolk country wines are on sale with a mouth-watering choice of fruit flavours, together with dandelion, cowslip and parsnip. There is a wide choice of other wines and malt whisky. The opening hours are 11 am to 3 pm and 6.30 pm to 11 pm and the usual Sunday times.

Telephone: 01493 700429.

How to get there: Reedham is on the B1140 to the south of Acle, which is halfway between Norwich and Great Yarmouth on the A47. Continue through the village on the B1140, following signs for the ferry.

Parking: There is parking at the pub or at various places in the village.

Length of the walk: About 4 miles. OS Landranger map 134 Norwich and the Broads (inn GR 407015).

The chain ferry taking three cars at a time across the river Yare is the focus of this walk. The nearby river bank offers lonely views across waving reeds to windmills and the great bulk of the Cantley beet factory in the far distance. In the summer, the scene is enlivened by boat traffic and sails. The route goes through grazing marshes criss-crossed by waterways and home to flocks of waterbirds (ducks, waders, snipe and swans) up to a hilly ridge overlooking the marshes and the river, thence back to Reedham village, over the railway and along the willow-lined road leading back to the ferry.

The Walk

Turn right out of the pub and go along the lane, passing the ferry on the left. Go up concrete steps and turn right along the bank. On one side are large reed beds hiding the river on the left and on the other a grassy tree-studded meadow with a pond, which is used by the pub in season as a mobile caravan and camping area. You can see a windmill ahead. Pass an old ferry ditched in reeds on the left and continue on past a wooden barrier opposite a ditch which bisects the water meadows on the right. The walk is gradually going round in a curve and occasionally you can see a small train making its way across the far end of the marshy grazing meadows and, further to the the left, the massive outline of the Cantley beet factory.

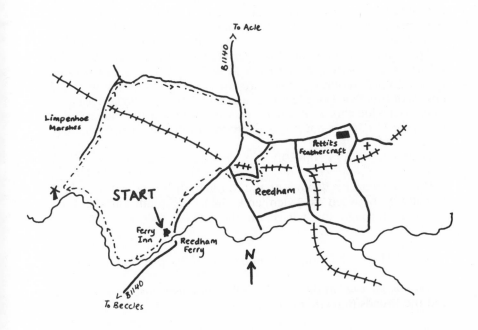

At a black-painted hut, the track along the river goes over a stile to the left, but this walk goes down the bank, passing the hut on the left, through (or over) the white-painted wooden gate ahead and down the grassy drove, which has water on either side and a row of electricity poles on the right. This is Limpenhoe Marshes. Go through a metal gate and along the drove, which can be churned up by cattle. Go through several gates, then through the gates over the level crossing of the railway, taking care to look out for trains. Carry on through a field along the edge of a ditch on the right. Go through more metal gates then straight up the track ahead, passing old red-brick cottages on the left. Continue ahead onto a road, passing farm buildings on the left, to a large grassy triangle just before a modern farmhouse.

Bear right up the lane here, and go right again, passing a red post box, to follow the lane back in the direction of Reedham along the spine of a gentle hill. Continue along the lane, then just past some houses on the left, at a T-junction, turn right, signposted to Reedham. The church tower appears over trees on the left. After a short distance on this rather busier road (Freethorpe Road), turn left down a lane, signposted to the church (Pottles Lane). Pass the village hall on the

View of Cantley beet factory, from Reedham.

right, then turn right down Witton Green by beautiful Pottles Barn ('1774' etched in brickwork on the eaves) and past Witton Close on the right. Bear left to the bridge over the railway, then turn right down a little road (The Havaker) running alongside the railway on the right, with houses and then the Railway Tavern (an excellent freehouse with good beers, food and accommodation) on the left. At a junction of roads, cross over and go down Ferry Road, which winds on through the marshes towards the ferry.

Places of interest nearby

Pettits Feathercraft, near the church, is signposted down a turning to the left before you reach the village of Reedham, as you come from Freethorpe. It is an animal adventure park with a miniature railway, exciting rides and lots of tame animals and birds, and a feathercraft workshop. Telephone: 01493 700094.

18 Earsham
The Queen's Head

This former coaching inn has stood by the village green for 400 years. It is a simple village pub with a beamed main bar and a copper hooded fire which offers welcome warmth in winter. The games room has pool and darts. There are a few tables on the hard standing outside, but more are in the beer garden, to the side of the pub, where barbecues are held in summer. The Queen's Head gives an excellent local service, including running the post office from one of its back rooms.

Two real ales (Courage Director's and Adnams Bitter) are kept and Beamish Irish stout is on draught. The lagers are Kronenbourg and Foster's. In addition there is John Smith's Bitter as well as Scrumpy Jack cider. Children are welcome and though there is no special room for them they do have their own menu (Kiddies Corner), which offers an inexpensive line in sausages, beefburgers, fish fingers or pizza – all with chips and peas or beans. The bar menu is fairly standard pub grub but again is excellent value. Vegetarian dishes, such as Chinese pancake rolls are on offer. There are toasted sandwiches and jacket potatoes with a choice of four fillings. Special dishes are added in summer and a take-away service is available.

Telephone: 01986 892623.

How to get there: Earsham, on the border between Norfolk and Suffolk, is just off the A143, a mile south-west of Bungay. The pub is at a crossroads in the centre of the village.

Parking: There is parking at the pub. Otherwise, you can park at the Otter Trust or in Bungay.

Length of the walk: About 3 miles (with an optional extension to the Otter Trust). There is a short cut. OS Landranger map 156 Saxmundham (inn GR 322891).

This walk starts in the small village of Earsham in the valley of the river Waveney on the borders of Suffolk. The whole area is full of history and the village was settled in Saxon times, though the church (some way from the present village and near the mill) stands on the site of a Roman encampment. The walk climbs the hill to Bungay first, to explore this interesting small town and its castle overlooking the river flood plain, before going through reed-fringed water meadows to Earsham church and mill. The walk can be extended by following the lane which leads to the Otter Trust, which has walking routes along the river.

The Walk

Go out of the pub to the left, cross over Station Road and continue down The Street, passing a garage on the left. Continue through the village without turning off, past the turning on the right to the mill. Just after the 30 mph delimit signs, the road goes over a waterway and continues on through open fields. There is a good view of Bungay church tower ahead. Go over a second bridge, ignoring the public footpath which goes to the right here, and continue on towards Bungay.

At the third road bridge, from which you can see Bungay Castle peeping out of the trees ahead, a short cut back to Earsham can be taken by turning to the right beyond the bridge and walking through fields to the mill. However, it would be a shame to miss out the interesting loop into Bungay.

For the main walk, cross over a narrow brick-built bridge into Earsham Street, which leads into the town, but almost immediately take a right turn down tiny Castle Lane. Pass between walled back gardens and where the lane forks take the right lower fork and continue on, soon passing through tangled greenery overlooking water meadows and osier beds on the right. The bank climbs steeply on the left and must have been part of the old castle fortifications. As the lane approaches houses go left up an alleyway. Note the Bigod Way arrow on a post here. This indicates the walking route circling Bungay and based on the castle, where there is an explanatory

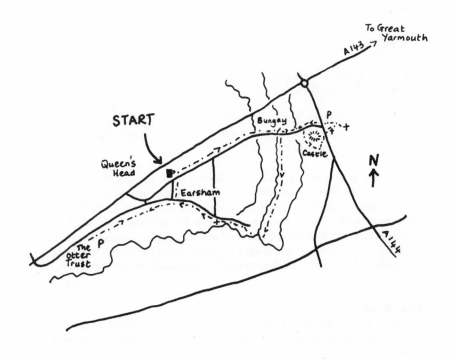

information board. Continue to climb alongside the old fortifications which are now Castle Hills play area with picnic tables. The path comes out on a road on a bend. Carry on to the left up the road. Past layby parking, a fingerpost points left to the castle, which is tucked away in an area of green grass behind wooden railings.

Go back to the road and turn left, going through an alley called Castle Orchard to the Swan pub on the left. From here is a view of the Buttercross, surmounted by the figure of Justice, rebuilt after a fire in the year 1688. Cross the road to visit redundant St Mary's church in its lovely graveyard with ruins beyond. This originally belonged to a Benedictine nunnery founded in 1160. The ornate Catholic church is next door. Walk through the churchyard towards grand red-brick Georgian houses beyond, where to the right is older Holy Trinity parish church with its Saxon tower set in an elevated position overlooking the valley. Return to Trinity Street and turn right to arrive at a little square. Cross over Bridge Street and Broad Street, with the Three Tuns pub on the corner, and then turn right down Earsham Street, with the Kings Head Hotel on the opposite side of the street.

Buttercross, Bungay.

Earsham Street's fine old buildings (many shops) make for a very lively street scene. Pass the White Lion pub and carry on downhill to recross the bridge at the entrance to Bungay.

At the next metal bridge, turn left (arrow marker) where the short cut went earlier. Go through a metal kissing gate to the right of a farm gate and walk down a broad track, with the river on the right and lovely views over to Bungay on the left. Go over a stile next to a metal gate, and continue on until the track peters out in a field. Keep on ahead alongside the river. Cross a stile (arrow marker) and continue on with a fence now on the left. Bear right over a wooden footbridge (arrow marker) and continue right along a narrow tree-lined path. This comes out onto a wider track, passing buildings on the left. Go over a humpy metal-barred bridge and continue on ahead. Ignore the footpaths to the Angles Way and the Bigod Way here. Continue on past cottages on the left and over a causeway by a ford past the commercial premises by the former mill and then All Saints' church with its fine iron railings, on the left. Ignore the road to the right and continue on to the next right turn up Milestone Lane, which leads back to the pub.

To reach the Otter Trust carry straight on for about a mile instead of turning up Milestone Lane.

Places of interest nearby

The *Otter Trust* has the world's largest collection of otters in natural river enclosures. Here British otters are bred for release into the wild. In addition, there are three lakes with a fine collection of European waterfowl, riverside walks and a tearoom and shop. Telephone: 01986 893470. *Bungay Castle* was built by Hugh Bigod in 1164. John Bigod added the round tower in 1294. The castle was in ruins by the 15th century and was owned by the Dukes of Norfolk who in the 20th century donated the castle to the town when restoration was undertaken. The *Angles Way* is a 77 mile walking route along the Waveney and Little Ouse valleys, linking Knettishall Heath near Thetford with Great Yarmouth.

Thetford
The Thomas Paine

This pleasant early Victorian hotel/pub has engulfed the small cottage where Thomas Paine, the famous or infamous late 18th century radical writer, was born. The hotel entrance, reached from the car park at the side, leads into a reception area decorated with Thomas Paine etchings and then upstairs to 13 en suite bedrooms. The long bar entered from the street has tables at the far end where children are welcome and doors leading into a lounge area and restaurant and also into an attractive small beer garden.

Real ales include Adnams Bitter, Stones and McEwans and there are two lagers on tap. You can have wines by the glass (there is a house wine) or there is a full wine list. Sandwiches are available all day. Bar food is served from 12 noon to 2 pm and from 6.30 pm to 9.30 pm and the menu is extremely comprehensive, with still further 'specials' advertised on a board. The restaurant takes only bookings at lunchtime, and is open from 7 pm to 9.30 pm in the evening. Last orders are at 10 pm on Fridays and Saturdays. An excellent table d'hôte menu is available and children can either have a half portion or choose from their own very full menu. The à la carte list offers a wide selection of delicious-sounding dishes and has plenty to tempt the vegetarian, including a mushroom and Stilton Stroganoff in a port and cream sauce. Meat eaters would find it hard to resist the sirloin steak Iceni with bacon and prawns in a cheese sauce. A special Sunday lunch menu has a wide variety of options. Would Thomas Paine have approved of all this luxury?

Telephone: 01842 755631.

How to get there: Thetford is on the south-west border of Norfolk on the A11. Follow signs from the bypass to the town centre. The Thomas Paine is in Whitehart Street, just off the A11.

Parking: The hotel has its own car park. There is a free car park further down the street or you could use any of the numerous central car parks. The castle and the priory, both a little way out of the centre, have their own parking.

Length of the walk: 2 miles which are suitable for wheelchairs or pushchairs, or a further extension can be taken along the river. OS Landranger map Thetford and Breckland (inn GR 832871).

There are no apologies for this being almost totally a town walk, because Thetford remains a fascinating and historic centre as it has been since the days of the Saxons when Offa was crowned here in AD 757. In the 11th century Thetford was a cathedral city and had five monasteries. The huge mound of Castle Hill was built after the Norman Conquest, although there are earlier defences from the Iron Age. The walk passes some interesting buildings in the town centre and then takes a pretty route along the river Little Ouse to Nuns' Bridges at a crossing of the Icknield Way before reaching Castle Hill. From here, a different but equally interesting route through the town leads to glorious Thetford Priory.

The Walk

Leave the hotel and walk down Whitehart Street, passing the King's Head pub, then the Ancient House museum (information centre). On the left is St Peter's church (known as the Black church due to the knapped flint on the tower) one of three surviving medieval churches in Thetford. It houses an exhibition of Thetford's history. At the crossroads go straight over, passing the Bell Hotel on the left. Just before the iron Town Bridge of 1829, turn left and walk alongside the Little Ouse river on the right through a modern paved area, passing an unusual triple bridge on the right. Continue on along a hard path next to a car park on the left.

Turn right along the path in front of the mill, which marks the limit of navigation on the Little Ouse. A mill has been on this site since Domesday and the present one, formerly a pit mill, ground coffee as

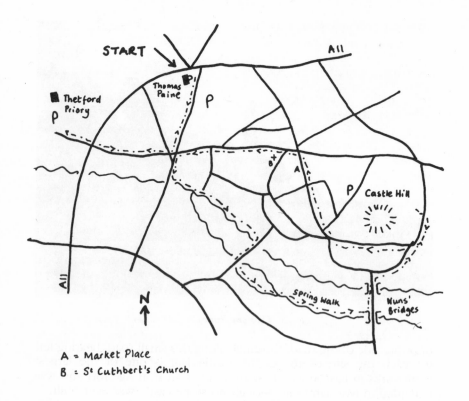

START

A11

Thomas Paine

P

Thetford Priory

P

B +

A

P Castle Hill

A11

N

Spring Walk

Nuns' Bridges

A = Market Place
B = St Cuthbert's Church

well as flour in the 19th century. Follow the path over a metal bridge and before a second metal bridge turn left along a narrow path leading through a grassy area, with the river on the left. After passing along a railinged causeway, the path bears left over a sluice gate and carries on, with the river now on the right, becoming Spring Walk, laid out in 1818 as a promenade for visitors to the spa. Spring House on the left was the Pump Room. Continue on towards an old stone bridge, one of the Nuns' Bridges (crossing the rivers Thet and Little Ouse) which once led to the Benedictine nunnery of St George, beyond the large green over the river on the right. This is now the headquarters of the British Trust for Ornithology, which has bird watching trails leading to flooded workings by the river.

Turn left along the road over the bridge and continue on to a second and then a third bridge. Beyond this, walk along a lovely old flint wall with an arch in it and turn right at the road junction near the Dolphin pub, with Ford Place, built on the site of an Augustinian friary, on the

Thetford Priory.

opposite side of the road. Continue along this small road, bearing left to reach the site of the castle. Castle Hill is one of the largest earthworks in East Anglia. It started out as an Iron Age fort and was extended in Norman times though no stone castle was ever built.

Return the way you came but bear right up Old Market Street, which contains some interesting old converted buildings including, on the right, Bidwell's brewery which closed in 1924. It was supplied by several large maltings by the river. The old gaol (rebuilt in 1796 and enlarged in 1816) on the left has two plaques showing leg and wrist irons. Continue on past the junction with Ford Street on the left to a road junction. Cross over and continue on down the road which leads eventually to the Market Place on the left. Here is the 'Thetford Grey' brick Guildhall, now an art centre, and nearby are the cast iron pillars of an old covered market shelter (The Shambles).

At the end of the Market Place cross the road and, keeping St Cuthbert's church on the left, continue down the pedestrianised King Street, passing the gold statue of Thomas Paine on the right, standing in front of King's House which was a royal hunting lodge. The flint walls of the garden behind are set with lovely pieces of old stone. Pass the Bell Hotel on the left, which used to be an important Elizabethan coaching inn on the main London to Norwich road. To visit the priory go straight ahead at the crossroads down Minstergate, passing the Charles Burrell museum. Use the underpass to arrive at the priory ruins. To extend the walk here go over grass beyond the car park to the river on the left and carry on to a bridge. Cross this and turn left to follow the other side of the bank back to town. This is an old haling path along which horses pulled barges. Alternatively, return down Minstergate and turn left up Whitehart Street back to the Thomas Paine.

Places of interest nearby

The *Cluniac Priory of St Mary* (English Heritage) was founded in 1103 by Sir Roger Bigod and the extensive buildings were constructed during the next few centuries. There is an impressive gatehouse and a two-storey prior's lodging as well as the ecclesiastical ruins. Telephone: 01842 766127. The *Charles Burrell Museum* is housed in some buildings belonging to the original steam traction engine company founded in 1770. Telephone: 01842 752599. The *Ancient House Museum* contains local and Breckland exhibits, including replicas of the Roman hoard found at Gallow's Hill (the originals are in the British Museum). A useful Thetford Walk leaflet full of historical detail can be bought here as well as a series of pamphlets, including one on Thomas Paine, and another on Prince Duleep Singh who gave this fine early 16th century timbered building to the town. Telephone: 01842 752599. *Thetford Forest Park* has Breckland walks and trails and cycle hire. Telephone: 01842 810271.

Bressingham
20 The Old Garden House

This large and lovely old pub caters for many requirements. From the patio and sheltered garden you enter a family room with old beams and a woodburning stove in an inglenook. There is plenty of seating at a long trestle surrounded by benches and at a pleasant old round table. A high chair stands ready for action. The main bar is long and beamed with, again, a woodburning stove and a flagged floor scattered with old rugs. The beautiful beamed restaurant features rugs, too.

The food is all freshly prepared and includes interesting dishes such as smoked pork fillet with apricot sauce. There are four different pies, including a vegetarian one, and a special large size can be ordered to share between four people. There is a bar menu on a board and daily specials, and the puddings are mainly old-fashioned favourites. The bar features guest ales of the month, for example Butcombe Bitter, Old Rooster Ale, Courage Best Bitter and Adnams Bitter. On draught are Beamish stout and Courage Dark Mild with Kronenbourg, Foster's and Miller Pilsner lagers and Scrumpy Jack cider. Opening hours are from 12 noon to 3 pm and 7 pm to 11 pm (10.30 pm on Sunday).

Telephone: 01379 687405.

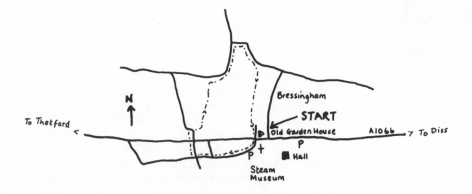

How to get there: The pub is on the main A1066 Thetford to Diss road, in the middle of Bressingham.

Parking: There is a large car park at the pub and parking at Bressingham Plant Centre and the Steam Museum.

Length of the walk: 2½ miles. A similar circuit can be done by wheelchairs and pushchairs by sticking to the lanes. OS Landranger map Thetford and Breckland (inn GR 077808).

The byways and lanes on the gentle agricultural slopes above Bressingham make for very pleasant walking, with lovely views down to the church and the pretty wooded valley of the river Waveney. Down in the valley are the attractive gardens associated with the Steam Museum and Plant Centre and glimpses of these can be seen from an ancient track. In summer fields along the main road blaze with colour from the blocks of herbaceous plants being brought on for the nursery.

The Walk

Wheelchairs and pushchairs would have to start off by going along the main road to the right. For others, leave the pub and cross the main road carefully, making for a lane which goes off to the right of the church of St John the Baptist. In summer this leads to the car park of the Bressingham Steam Museum (out of season parking is at the Plant Centre). Follow this little lane as it bears right, passing scattered dwellings. The river Waveney, the boundary between Norfolk and Suffolk, runs in the wooded valley beyond the gardens of Bressingham Hall on the left. The tarmaced lane becomes a wide, grassy track carrying on through fields and fens, then past cottages on the right. At one stage the lane goes over a ford with a small footbridge to the right of it. At a crossroads of green tracks carry straight on through hedges to a spinney on the right. Eventually the track comes out through a white gate by the entry to Three Gates Farm (signposted 'Angles Way'). Bear right at this junction of ways to reach the main road.

Cross carefully and walk up the small road opposite (Halford Lane). Soon there is a public footpath signpost pointing right just before a bend in the road (or continue up the lane here). Follow this and walk along the edge of the field, keeping a deep ditch on the right, then bear left by the public footpath signpost on the corner of the field and walk up the boundary again, with a deep ditch and also a hedge on the right. Go on to the corner of this field near a metal gate. To the left of this is a footbridge by a post with arrow markers on. Cross this, keeping ahead, and walk up a hedgerow with trees in on the right and an open field on the left. Come out on a tiny lane at a wooden footpath signpost.

Turn right past farm buildings on the right and a lovely old pantiled house with a crow-stepped gable on the left. The lane (called The Valley) goes uphill with a copse on the right. Soon after this a public footpath signpost points across a field on the right. This can be taken to cut the corner off if a path is left through crops – make for a red-brick house and the path comes out to the left of this. If not, carry

Steam Museum, Bressingham.

95

on up the lane and bear right at the next junction by lovely old cream-washed Fenner's Farm. Ignore the road to the left and walk along the lane towards houses. The lane bears right at cottages, past pretty thatched High House on the left. Turn off the road onto a footpath to the right, just past Poplar Farm.

Otherwise, go further on to the road junction near houses and a war memorial and turn right down the lane here. This leads past the school on the right down to meet the main road, where a right turn leads back to the pub.

The field footpath goes along a narrow conifer-lined path on the left-hand boundary of a garden and bungalow. Go onto an overgrown path to the left of a pile of farm rubbish and down into a field (arrow markers). Keep ahead across the field (there may be no marked path) for a shortish distance towards a grass baulk running at right angles, dividing the fields. Jump the ditch here and turn left along the grassy baulk (with a ditch on the left) to a wooden post with arrow markers on it. Turn right here and follow the wide, grassy baulk (with a ditch again on the left) round the edge of the field to emerge by a gate onto a track, with a few dwellings on the left. Carry on a little way to the road and turn left back to the pub.

Places of interest nearby

The *Bressingham Plant Centre* (Bloom's of Bressingham). This 2 acre garden centre and tearoom is open from 10.30 am to 5.30 pm every day except Christmas and Boxing Day. Special demonstrations and gardening talks are arranged. There is a huge 500 acre nursery spread out along the main road. The *Steam Museum* (a comprehensive collection of British and Continental locomotives and various tracks) and adjoining gardens are administered independently by Bressingham Steam Museum Trust. Alan Bloom's Dell Garden is in the grounds of Georgian Bressingham Hall. For opening times telephone 01379 687386. Adrian Bloom's garden 'Foggy Bottom' is generally open on the first Sunday in each month and on Mondays from April to October. The *Angles Way* is a 77 mile walking route from Knettishall Heath near Thetford to Great Yarmouth.